"Please don't read th. immensely practical, and loaded with amazing insight. If you follow even a few of the suggestions Susan has brilliantly articulated, my executive coaching business is in jeopardy. Don't tell your friends about it either."
JOHN FICKEN, PHD
CEO, THE QUOTIDIAN GROUP

"The exercises and advice in this book helped me identify and cultivate professional strengths that I did not even know I had."
SUE STEINKAMP, MANAGER PSYCHOMETRIC SERVICES, PEARSON.VUE

"This book should be in every working woman's arsenal. The parable of Phoebe fish (Chapter 6) is a must read! It helped me gain valuable insight into my own career as well as being a fun story for me to share with my three young daughters."
NIKKI SHEPHERD EATCHEL, VICE PRESIDENT TEST DEVELOPMENT, PROMETRIC

"I wish I'd had this book when I was earlier in my career. Susan's advice and reflective activities make you stop and consider what's really important to you in your career and in your life."
TERRI FOLEY, DIGITAL PROJECTS DIRECTOR, COUGHLAN COMPANIES

HOW TO BECOME SUCCESSFUL

Without

BECOMING A MAN

◇◇

THE WORKING WOMAN'S GUIDE TO
Success, Sanity, Leadership & Life

◇◇

SUSAN DAVIS-ALI, PhD

To order additional copies of this book, contact:
Xlibris Corporation 1-888-795-4274 www.Xlibris.com
Orders@Xlibris.com
48882

◇◇

To my children, Kate and Andrew
WHO ARE THE REASON I CREATE SANITY IN MY LIFE

&

To my husband Jeff Ali
WHO IS AN UNWAVERING CHAMPION OF MY PROFESSIONAL SUCCESS

◇◇

Foreword
A LETTER TO THE READER

Dear Professional Women:

Many of us approach our careers the same way we'd approach a new board game that was given to us without directions. We play with enthusiasm. We do our best to figure things out as we go along. We take our cues from the other players. We look carefully for subtle clues that might reveal the rules. We know we'd have a better time playing if we just had a copy of the directions, but we can't seem to find them.

> • For decades, men seem to have been given a copy of the directions. This book is my way of giving the directions to working women.

You probably picked up this book with some combination of curiosity, skepticism, and enthusiasm. You're intrigued about the possibility of creating greater success and sanity in your life, but you're wondering how you'll find the time to read the book, let alone implement the strategies. Good news! I kept that in mind when I created this book.

- This book was written specifically for busy working women. It's an easy-to-read guidebook, not a dense novel.

- The book begins with a summary of the chapters so you decide which ones meet your immediate interests and needs.

- The chapters contain quizzes and exercises that engage you in the information presented.

- The strategies are things you can begin implementing today.

In this book, I address you as an individual, under your own circumstances. The advice I share with you is not a "one-size fits all" model. It puts your goals and interests at the center of the equation. I help you define what success and sanity mean to you within the context, constraints, and opportunities of your own life. I show you how to put a plan in place to help you achieve the goals that you have for yourself.

As professional women, I believe we are each unique. We have different job titles, work for different organizations, come from different backgrounds, have different personalities, and bring to the table a variety of different goals and aspirations.

Regardless of all that, we share a lot in common:

- We enjoy our jobs on most days, and tolerate them on others.

- We are looking to be authentic in who we are.

- We are not looking for success at any cost.

- We bring a female perspective to everything we do.

- We typically work in organizations that we do not own.

- We want satisfaction in our careers and our lives.

- We want to be the very best we can be.

I'm here to tell you that the life you imagine for yourself is possible! You've taken your first step toward greater success and sanity by opening this book. The next steps are waiting for you in the chapters ahead.

All my best,

CONTENTS

Foreword: A Letter to the Reader   i

Introduction: Chapter Previews   ix

Chapter 1:   It's Not About Being Perfect,   1
              It's About Being Real

Chapter 2:   Starting on the Road to Success and Sanity   13

Chapter 3:   Three Simple Secrets That Will Change Your Life   39
              If you read nothing else, read this chapter.

Chapter 4:   Five Fundamental Truths About Business   51

Chapter 5:   Making Smart Career Choices: 65
               A Reality Check

Chapter 6:   The Parable of Phoebe Fish: 89
               The Big Fish Little Pond Effect

Chapter 7:   Six Degrees of Separation   113
               in Organizations

Chapter 8:   Corporate Culture: 123
               What's the Right Fit for You?

Chapter 9:   The Linear Career Track: 145
               Is It Your Only Option?

Chapter 10:   A Great Job in a Bad Organization   161
               Equals a Bad Job

Chapter 11:   Creating Your Authentic Career   169

Chapter 12:   Attitude is Everything   183
               During Times of Change

Chapter 13:   Inspirational Leadership   191

Chapter 14:   Lessons Learned From   201
              My Biggest Mistakes

Chapter 15:   Managing Your Mommy Guilt   217

Chapter 16:   What's Being Female Got to Do With It?   245

Appendix A: Chapter Reviews   251

Appendix B: Recommended Reading List   259

Appendix C: Acknowledgements   271

Appendix D: About the Author   275

Introduction
CHAPTER PREVIEWS

I recognize the time limitations that working women face. Therefore, I designed each chapter as a stand-alone coaching session – to be read in whatever order is of greatest interest and relevance to you.

The brief chapter previews presented below are designed to help you determine the chapters that may be most immediately valuable.

Chapters 1 and 2 establish the foundation for all other chapters, so I highly recommend you begin with those.

CHAPTER 1 It's Not About Being Perfect, It's About Being Real

This chapter questions the notion of work/life balance and proposes instead the concepts of success and sanity. It focuses on the differences between being perfect and being real.

CHAPTER 2 Starting on the Road to Success and Sanity

This chapter introduces the concepts of success and sanity that serve as the foundation for the entire book. It contains the Leadhership1™ Success and Sanity Quiz.

CHAPTER 3 Three Simple Secrets That Will Change Your Life

This chapter outlines three simple secrets that will change your life. It focuses on tips for creative time management as well as strategies for creating greater sanity in your important relationships.

CHAPTER 4 Five Fundamental Truths About Business

This chapter discusses five fundamental truths about business that applies to all types of organizations. It contains quizzes and exercises to test your adherence to these truths.

CHAPTER 5 Making Smart Career Choices: A Reality Check

This chapter presents a reality check – an honest and realistic evaluation of where you are now in your career, and where you want to be 2-3 years from now.

There is a quiz designed to help you see how your strengths and weaknesses are perceived by an employer. You are then better prepared to make smart career choices for yourself.

CHAPTER 6 The Parable of Phoebe Fish

This chapter explores the big fish/little pond effect through the whimsical character of Phoebe Fish. This parable gets you thinking about what size fish you want to be in your career and what size pond you prefer to swim in. An exercise is included to help guide your thinking.

CHAPTER 7 Six Degrees of Separation in Organizations

This chapter outlines the importance of your position on the organizational chart. It references the popular game "Six Degrees of Kevin Bacon" to demonstrate how the distance between you and the CEO determines your power and influence at work.

The exercise at the end of this chapter helps you consider which degree of separation in your various jobs has brought you the greatest satisfaction.

CHAPTER 8 Corporate Culture: What's the Right Fit for You?

This chapter examines an organization's personality which is commonly referred to as its culture. Seven characteristics of corporate culture are presented including: Communication Style, Leadership Style, Focus, Values, Flexibility, Rewards, and Pace.

The chapter contains a quiz that shows each personality characteristic along a continuum. By examining the characteristics that you value the most in an organization, the quiz helps you determine which type of culture is the right fit for you.

CHAPTER 9 The Linear Career Track: Is It Your Only Option?

This chapter is a follow-up to Chapter 8. It addresses the question of whether or not a woman's career track always has to be linear.

CHAPTER 10 A Great Job in a Bad Organization Equals a Bad Job

This chapter argues that there is no such thing as a great job in a bad company. It shows how a great job in a bad company almost always turns into a bad job over time.

CHAPTER 11 Creating Your Authentic Career

This chapter examines the notion of what it means to have an authentic career. It emphasizes the importance of considering your interests and not just your abilities in choosing a career that will bring you success and sanity.

It includes a quiz to help you identify whether your current career feels authentic to you.

CHAPTER 12 Attitude is Everything During Times of Change

This chapter introduces the concept of job change and discusses the importance of your attitude during organizational change.

CHAPTER 13 Inspirational Leadership

This chapter looks at 20 qualities of great leadership from a female perspective. It reminds everyone that leadership can and should happen at every level of an organization.

The exercise directs you to pick 10 characteristics that you value the most in leaders and compares these to your own strongest leadership characteristics.

CHAPTER 14 Lessons Learned from My Biggest Mistakes

This chapter reveals four of my biggest professional mistakes and the lessons I learned from them so you can avoid them.

CHAPTER 15 Managing Your Mommy Guilt

This chapter is written specifically for working moms. It examines the issue of mommy guilt that will be alive and well as long as there are working moms.

The chapter offers several helpful suggestions that come directly from working moms about how they successfully manage their guilt. There are numerous exercises throughout this chapter.

CHAPTER 16 What's Being Female Got to Do With It?

This chapter answers the question of what being female has to do with it. It also contains some final thoughts about how you can take action after reading this book.

QUIZZES AND EXERCISES

Many of the chapters contain quizzes and exercises, and I strongly encourage you to engage in them. If you don't want to write in the book, additional forms can be printed out at **www.leadhership1. com**

chapter

It's Not About Being Perfect, It's About Being Real

Just for the record, I think men are terrific. This book is not about what's wrong with men: it's about what's right with women. I adore my husband, brother, father, male colleagues, and friends. My enthusiasm doesn't come from excluding men, it comes from including women.

Pick up the most recent copy of *Harvard Business Review, Pink Magazine, Working Mother,* or the *Catalyst Report* and you'll find compelling reasons why women's leadership is more important than ever. The country's corporate workforce is facing a shortage of qualified leaders, while at the same time high-performing women are leaving the workforce in record numbers. Not only do we need women leaders in the workforce for sheer numbers alone, but for the diversity of thought and action that they bring to the table.

WHAT THE RESEARCH SAYS

Research now suggests that the differences in hormones and how the female brain is wired may result in many of the workplace qualities that women – in contrast to the typical man – often exhibit. These include a holistic approach to decision-making and problem solving, awareness of subtle body language, reliance on intuition, proven ability for multi-tasking, and a more inclusive management style (*Pink*, August/September 2007).

With that said, corporate America still rewards attributes more likely to be male than female, such as a linear approach to problem solving, focusing on one task at a time, and top-down decision making. High achieving female professionals have often adopted male behaviors in order to gain the respect and recognition they desire, and you can hardly blame them. However, by becoming more like men, women have failed to promote the female attributes noted above that women leaders have to offer an organization.

The reality is that the corporate world is still predominately governed by male rules, so it's important for professional women to understand these rules. Understanding them is different than letting them totally change who you are. Like the title of this book says, it's about becoming successful **without** becoming a man.

MY PERSPECTIVE

Everyone looks at life from their own perspective and I am no different. This book is not without bias, opinion, or judgment, so I think it's only fair to present my perspective up front.

After receiving my PhD in Social Psychology from The University of Michigan, I went to work for a large test development company. We developed and published multiple-choice tests that were used by psychologists and health care providers to diagnose a variety of psychological disorders.

My new corporate environment gave me a huge pool of fascinating people to observe, and observing is what social psychologists love most to do. I observed people at all levels of the organization: how they dressed, where they went for lunch, whom they talked to in the halls, and how they conducted themselves in meetings. I watched, and I watched, and I watched.

It did not take me long to figure out that being male and being white greatly increased your chances of being successful in business. Men had offices; women had cubicles. Oddly, the few women who did have offices looked an awful lot like the men who had offices. Everything about these women screamed, "Please do not notice that I am female!"

I offer observations from more than 10 years in various corporate settings. I've spent the majority of my life being a successful female with an emphasis on being both "successful" and "female".

I decided that these women must all be in on a little secret - act like you're a man if you want to get ahead. I was sure that at the end of the day, these women turned off the "act" and become female again. After months of observing these top women, I had a sinking feeling that perhaps I was wrong. I started to suspect that these women were not just pretending to be men, but had actually become just like men on their way up the corporate ladder.

Was it possible that the women who started out more like men were the ones actually chosen for the executive positions? Maybe being like a man was a prerequisite for the top jobs.

The thought was both horrifying and depressing to me. I knew if this was what it took to be successful, I was doomed. I knew if starting out like a man was the secret, then I was doomed too.

BEING WHO YOU ARE

In high school, I was president of my class while also being captain of the cheerleading squad. In college, I was a

Phi Beta Kappa scholar while also being actively involved in a social sorority. In graduate school, I wore sweaters and skirts to class, much to the confusion of my blue-jean wearing colleagues.

Years later, as I embarked on my first professional job, I knew I had no interest in or ability to radically change who I was. I looked at the successful woman role models in the corporate world and wondered if I stood a chance of doing things a different way. Could I be true to who I am and meet the ambitious career goals I had set out for myself? Had other women done it before me and if so, what insights could they offer me? Was there really any chance of becoming successful without becoming a man?

The short answer is yes. The longer answer lies within the chapters of this book. My story has a happy ending, and yours can, too. Many of the successful women that I worked with over the years are nothing at all like men. They are mothers, daughters, wives, partners, and friends.

They are smart, energetic, and enthusiastic about both their careers and their lives. They bring their personalities as well as their problem solving skills to work with them everyday. They do not apologize for being feminine, yet they do not exploit being feminine for their own personal gain. They embrace all that is successful and all that is female. They integrate their lives into their work. They are strong inspirational women who make strong inspirational leaders.

> **SUCCESS =** Your ability to achieve your career goals
>
> **SANITY =** Your ability to truly enjoy your life

THE MYTH OF WORK/LIFE BALANCE

This book is not a recipe for work/life balance. I have yet to meet a successful working woman who feels she has found a true balance in her life. The successful women I know have found what seems more appropriately referred to as "success and sanity."

To quote Kerrii Anderson, former CEO of Wendy's, "I prefer the word 'integration.' If you use the word 'balance', you're misconstruing what your life is going to be like." (*Pink*, August/September 2007).

Work/life balance sounds great, but it's just not real. In reality, I can't think of many working women who have work/life balance. The phrase oversimplifies the ability to "have it all" which most working women feel is painfully beyond their grasp. The working women I know are striving for sanity in their busy lives, not balance. Thus, I choose to focus on sanity.

> Work/life balance is a wonderful ideal,
> but success and sanity are realistic goals.

So what does the notion of sanity look like compared to work/life balance? If you're a working woman, you already know the answer to this question even if you can't quite articulate it.

- Balance implies packing a nutritious home-cooked meal for your lunch. Sanity means eating lunch out of the company vending machine.

- Balance implies you never go to bed with dirty dishes in your sink. Sanity means you do the dishes only when the sink is overflowing.

- Balance implies that you have your life under control. Sanity means that you're happy when you are one step ahead of the next crisis.

Success and sanity come together in a sometimes off-balanced, but manageable way that works differently for each individual woman. Success and sanity do not come without effort, and they often do not come without assistance.

THE NEED FOR MENTORS

I have been extremely fortunate to have excellent mentors and coaches throughout my career, and frankly very few women find success and sanity without them. As my own career advanced, I felt a strong responsibility to mentor the next generation of leaders. I was fortunate to be part of an organization that allowed me to do that.

In today's competitive corporate environment, finding members of upper management with time to mentor and coach emerging women leaders is increasingly difficult.

Companies utilize their top talent to perform the much-needed executive level roles while trying to simultaneously cultivate the talented leaders of tomorrow. It's not an easy undertaking and research tells us that most companies are failing. Successful women leaders continue to leave corporate American in droves. (The Hidden Brain Drain:. Off-Ramps and On-Ramps in Women's Careers – *Harvard Business Review Research Report,* March 2005).

I believe that many of the top women who leave the fast track do so because they lack role models within their organization who look like they do with regard to age, gender, race, and marital status. If you can't see yourself among the leadership of your organization, then you fail to see your own potential within that organization.

This book is not written at the exclusion of men, it's written for the inclusion of women. It's written for women who are searching for a mentor and a coach. It is written for women who are striving to become business leaders, but not at the expense of losing who they are.

I draw upon my PhD in social psychology when applicable as a foundation for helping to explain why people think and behave the way they do in the corporate world. Understanding human nature is a strong foundation to good leadership.

While the roots of this book are definitely grounded in the for-profit business model, I have coached women in not-for-profit, academic, and legal settings as well. They tell me that the strategies I present hold true for them, too.

The strategies in this book are not geared toward making radical changes in the male-dominated corporate culture. They are about facing and embracing both the reality and the opportunities presented to working women in today's business world. The book is about helping you navigate your own chosen career path more effectively.

BEING REAL

As high-aspiring, high-achieving women in the workplace, you have undoubtedly met obstacles and naysayers along your way. They will tell you that women can't have it all, and that may be true, especially if having it all means fulfilling someone else's expectations. But what if you get to decide what having it all means? What if you're able to create a life for yourself in which success and sanity are not only possible, but highly probable?

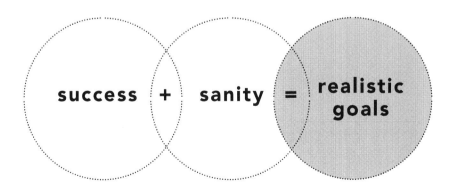

success + sanity = realistic goals

Having it all (by my definition) is not about reaching for someone else's ideal. It's not about living up to someone else's standards. It's about integrating who you are as a person and who you are as a professional into one successful and sane life.

This book is designed to help you discover where you are now and where you want to be, and shows you how to get there most effectively. Having it all is not about being perfect – it's about being real. Real women, real lives, real success, real sanity. **Join us!**

chapter

Starting on the Road to Success and Sanity

In the timeless classic *The Wizard of Oz,* Dorothy knows exactly what she must do to reach her goals – she has to follow the yellow brick road. Things are not quite as prescribed for today's working women. There are no easily identifiable yellow brick roads for us to follow. We are responsible for creating our own pathways toward success and sanity. So let's begin.

Take a minute to imagine your ideal life – what would it look like? Would you choose to be a professional working woman or would you forgo the working world? Would you have more career success than you currently have or, possibly, less? Would you strive for greater sanity in your life or are you content with the sanity that you have?

If you are like most incredibly busy working women, you've already glossed over these hypothetical questions in search of the concrete coaching strategies that I promised you were in this book.

I admire that about you. You are goal-oriented and you don't want to waste time and energy on life's "what-ifs". These qualities makes you well-suited for the corporate world where tasks and deliverables are the name of the game and the luxury of time is rarely on your side.

However, these qualities do not necessarily make you well-suited for success and sanity in your own life. I challenge you to slow down for just a minute. Don't think of these hypothetical questions as merely another task on your "to do" list.

I respect your need for efficiency, really I do. These questions, like other aspects of success and sanity, require you to think, reflect, and digest – three words that are not well-aligned with the" do, do, do" philosophy of the busy working woman.

Success and sanity will be your reward if you allow yourself to truly engage in the program (including the quizzes and exercises) outlined in this book. This program is not all that different than any physical exercise program you might embark on, the results do not happen without a certain degree of discipline and commitment.

What if you can't commit to participating in the entire program, should you just give up now? No! Read the chapter previews at the beginning of this book and make a commitment to engage in the chapters that address your most pressing needs.

If you think I don't understand your hectic life, I do. I've lived the fast pace for many, many years. I've probably done most of the crazy things you've done to juggle success and sanity. And because I have done them, I fully understand why you are doing them too. I promise you I will keep the discussions on point and be respectful of your limited time.

The coaching in this book is designed to be very concrete and very hands-on. Like most development programs, we need to start by answering the questions "Where am I now and where do I want to be?" The quizzes on the following pages are designed to help you assess your success and sanity today, as well as benchmark where you want it to be in the future.

SUCCESS PLUS SANITY

Success and sanity are intersecting pathways that, together, create your life. They are not parallel tracks.
When both run smoothly, life is good.
When one falls apart, the other tends to follow.

WHAT IS SUCCESS AND WHY DOES IT MATTER?

In general, success is a measure of how closely your current career is meeting your career goals – the closer the match, the greater your success.

Success is specifically defined as having the job you want within an organization you enjoy, while achieving the professional rewards and recognition that you desire.

- **The job** itself includes everything from day-to-day responsibilities, to job title, to your place on the organizational chart.

- **The organization** includes everything from the reputation of the organization, to the culture, to your boss, your direct reports, and your colleagues.

- **Financial Rewards** includes everything from salary, to bonuses, to benefits.

- **Professional Recognition** includes non-tangible things such as leadership opportunities, intellectual challenge, professional recognition, and job stability.

The benchmark of success is not absolute. There is no gold standard of success that all women subscribe to. A career as a project manager in a large corporation might define success to one woman, while being the COO of a not-for-profit might define success to another. One woman's definition of success may be another woman's definition of failure.

Similarly, the importance of success is not absolute. Success matters only in so much as it matters to you. For some women, success means everything and for others, it's far less important. Some women define themselves by their success, others do not. Knowing how you feel about success is important because success can either detract from your sanity, or promote your sanity, depending on the value you place on it.

BE CAREFUL WHAT YOU WISH FOR

Success begets success. What this means is that once you achieve initial success you may find that more opportunities for success come your way. Why is that?

Most companies and organizations have a list of high potential employees. They call these employees "rising stars," future leaders or a variety of different names, but the concept remains the same. It's a list of employees considered to have the raw talent needed to succeed.

Some companies make these lists public thus creating a sort of open competition among employees. Other companies only notify the people on the list as a more private reward and recognition, while some companies keep the names on the list completely secret. Regardless of the level of publicity, the people on this list are the first ones tapped for new important opportunities and once they prove themselves as a success in that role, they get tapped again. Rising stars often find themselves on a fast-paced career track.

Sounds terrific, right? Not necessarily. Success rarely comes without a price and the price can be a reduction in your sanity. Success can be very demanding of your time and as your free time decreases, so can your sanity. Success can mean more time spent at the office, more time spent traveling to see clients, or simply more time spent thinking about work. With only 24 hours in a day, more time at work means less time away from work.

However, success does not mandate a reduction in sanity. Many very successful women have created sanity in their lives. We'll talk about specific strategies to help you do that in subsequent chapters, but for now, let's accept that it's possible.

It is possible for successful women to leave work, turn off their cell phones, laptops, Blackberries, or newest communication gadgets designed to help them stay connected 24/7. It is possible, but it's easier said than done. While we can turn off the electronic devices, it's sometimes much harder to turn off our brains and to stop thinking about work.

Some women reluctantly think about work after they leave the office because they don't have a strategy in place to turn the thinking off. Other women choose to think about work when they leave the office because they find

With only 24 hours in a day,

more time at work means less time away from work.

7 am

Start Work

6 pm

Leave Work

it mentally energizing. This level of constant engagement with work can have an impact on sanity. It's a trade-off. The trade-off of sanity for success is completely reasonable, necessary, and admirable for some very high achieving women.

The only downside to the trade-off is if it becomes emotionally or physically unhealthy. Success is not intrinsically good or bad. Its value is for you to decide.

However, if success causes harm to you or your family, you need to re-evaluate your career goals sooner rather than later. No amount of success is worth a complete loss of sanity.

What if you are not energized by your success? What if your success drains you? What if the demands of your current job seem more problematic than they are worth? What if you've lost your sanity because of your success? If any of these describe you, then it's possible that you've become more successful than you really want to be.

Odd as it may sound, this can happen. A woman's ability should never dictate her ambition. A woman's ability to become high achieving does not necessitate that she become high achieving. Each woman must decide for herself what level of success and sanity is right for her.

WHAT IS SANITY AND WHY DOES IT MATTER?

Sanity is a measure of your ability to truly enjoy your life. Sanity is specifically defined as having the time, the energy, the financial resources, and the relationships that you want in your life in order to be able to enjoy your life.

- **Time** means having time for family and friends, and having time to participate in the activities and hobbies that interest you.

- **Energy** means having both the physical and emotional energy you need to pursue your non-career goals.

- **Financial Resources** means having the money to pay your bills and do the things you enjoy in life.

- **Relationships** means having the people in your life with whom you want to have meaningful relationships – spouse, partner, children, friends, or family.

As with success, there is no gold standard of sanity that all women agree on. For one woman, eating fast food while driving home from work constitutes sanity. For another woman, sanity means stopping at the grocery store after work to pick up fresh ingredients so she can cook one of her favorite meals.

Similarly, the importance of sanity is not absolute. For some women, it means everything and for others it's far less importance. For the women who highly value sanity, they never want to appear overwhelmed or out of control. Sanity is very important to their self-image.

For other women, the appearance of sanity is far less important. They are fine with people seeing them struggle a bit to keep their head above water. The perception of sanity is far less important to them.

Knowing how you feel about sanity is an important variable because sanity can either detract from your success, or promote your success, depending on how much you value it.

Sanity is best defined through the eye of the beholder. I remember thinking my life was fairly sane until the time my in-laws came to stay with us for a week. I should preface this by saying that I have the world's best in-laws. However, I can honestly say that I saw a look of absolute horror on their faces every night, as they watched the rhythm and pace of our normal evening routine unfold.

THE ROUTINE WENT SOMETHING LIKE THIS:

5:15 pm	**Leave the office – hope I'm not late.**
5:30 pm	**Arrive at daycare – pick up son.**
6:00 pm	**Arrive at school – pick up daughter.**
6:30 pm	**Dinner, then clean kitchen.**
7:30 pm	**Pack lunches for next day. Feed dogs.**
7:45 pm	**Spend time together as a family.**
8:15 pm	**Get kids ready for bed – bath, books, bed.**
8:45 pm	**Do housework, exercise, or simply decompress.**
9:30 pm	**Read e-mails, finish up work.**
11:00 pm	**Go to bed - on a good night.**

Most of the time the schedule ran smoothly and we felt comfortable with it. However, from my in-laws perspective, our lives looked like absolute chaos. They did their best to hide their concern from us, but I could see it.

Looking back on this routine, I can see why it felt pretty sane to us, if not to them. Our kids were young. There was no homework yet and no after-school activities. Now that our kids are older, I've come to appreciate that our sanity expectations need to shift. Now we have homework and after school activities to add to our evening routine.

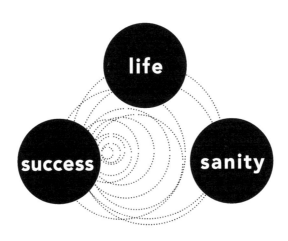

SANITY IS WHAT YOU MAKE IT

At the end of the day, no one can tell you what sanity looks like. It is yours to define. If you are a wife, a mom, a community leader, a political activist, a sports enthusiast, or a travel fanatic, sanity means being able to participate in these roles in a way that is rewarding and meaningful to you.

Sanity is about living your life in a way that is acceptable to you, although probably not ideal to you. Sanity is not about perfection. It's not about living up to some unattainable societal norms. It's about making peace with the never-ending juggling act in your life.

For most of us work/life balance is a lofty unattainable ideal. Sanity is a reasonable compromise for having our success and "eating" it too. Sanity is what we settle for, strive for, hope for, and eventually learn to accept as successful working women.

THE SUCCESS
AND SANITY
QUIZ

Introduction: The Success and Sanity Quiz is an important first step in helping you achieve your personal and professional goals. The quiz is a snapshot of your current goals versus your reality. It provides an overview of "what you have" versus "what you want."

In some cases your goals may exceed your reality, in other cases your reality may meet or exceed your goals. The quiz will help highlight this very clearly for you. Your results are based on what's important to you, not what's important to anyone else. Your goals and your priorities determine your results.

The quiz is also designed to help you turn emotions into tangible targets. For example, if you are feeling frustrated at work and don't know why, it's hard to develop an action plan to reduce your frustration. However, if the quiz helps you discover that your frustration is related to some unmet financial goals, then you have a tangible target to go after.

The quiz is divided into two parts. **Part I** provides a general overview of your success and sanity. **Part II** explores specific components of your success and sanity.

PART I Examines your OVERALL success and sanity.

Directions: Complete Steps A through C below. Descriptions for the values 0 and 10 are provided as a guide to illustrate the meaning of the scale's endpoints.

OVERALL SUCCESS

A. On the 0 to 10 scale presented below, CIRCLE the number that best represents your CURRENT LEVEL of success.
0 = I have not achieved any of my career goals.
10 = I have achieved all of my career goals.

0 . . . .1 . . . .2 . . . . 3 . . . . 4 . . . .5 . . . .6 . . . . 7 . . . . 8 . . . .9 10

B. On the same 0 to 10 scale, go back and place a SQUARE around the number that best represents your GOALS for success.

C. Your GAP Score is the difference between the number in the CIRCLE and the number in the SQUARE.

My Gap Score for OVERALL SUCCESS = ☐

Gap Scores can range from -10 to +10. The direction (+ or -) is important. Check the box below for the direction of your Gap score.

☐ The number I selected in the square is larger than the number I selected in the circle.

▶ This is a negative gap. A negative gap indicates that you want greater success than you currently have. It represents unmet goals.

☐ The number I selected in the circle is larger than the number I selected in the square.

▶ This is a positive gap. A positive gap indicates that your current success exceeds your goals. It represents a surplus of success.

☐ The number I selected in the circle is the same as the number I selected in the square.

▶ This is no gap. A gap score of zero indicates that you currently have the success you desire. It represents consistency between your goals and your reality.

A. On the 0 to 10 scale presented below, CIRCLE the number that best represents your CURRENT LEVEL of sanity.

0 = I have no sanity. I am completely unable to enjoy my life.10 = I have total sanity. I am completely able to enjoy my life.

0 . . . .1 . . . . .2 . . . . 3 . . . . 4 . . . .5 . . . . .6 . . . . 7 . . . . 8 . . . .9 10

B. On the same 0 to 10 scale, go back and place a SQUARE around the number that best represents your sanity GOALS.

C. The Gap Score is the difference between the number in the CIRCLE and the number in the SQUARE. Calculate your Gap Score.

My Gap Score for OVERALL SANITY = ☐

Gap Scores can range from -10 to +10. The direction (+ or -) is important. Check the box below for the direction of your Gap score.

☐ The number I selected in the square is larger than the number I selected in the circle.

▶ This is a negative gap. A negative gap indicates that you want greater sanity than you currently have. It represents unmet goals.

☐ The number I selected in the circle is larger than the number I selected in the square.

▶ This is a positive gap. A positive gap indicates that your current sanity exceeds your goals. It represents a surplus of sanity.

☐ The number I selected in the circle is the same as the number I selected in the square.

▶ This is no gap. A gap score of zero indicates that you currently have the sanity you desire. It represents consistency between your goals and your reality.

• Remember to indicate whether it's a positive or negative gap.

PART II Examines four specific components of your success and four specific components of your sanity.

FOUR COMPONENTS OF SUCCESS

Directions: Answer questions 1 through 4 below. For each of the questions with a 0 to 10 rating scale, use the following guidelines:

0 = It does not match at all.
10 = It's a complete match.

1a. How closely does your current JOB POSITION match what you are ideally looking for in a job position? Job position includes everything from your actual job title to your day-to-day job responsibilities.

0 . . . .1. . . . .2. . . . 3 . . . . 4 . . . .5. . . . .6. . . . 7 . . . . 8 . . . .9. . . . 10

1b. When you think about your success, how important is your JOB POSITION? **Check one box.**

☐ Very Important
☐ Somewhat Important
☐ Not Very Important

2a. How closely does your current ORGANIZATION match what you are ideally looking for in an organization? Organization includes everything from the company culture, to your colleagues, to your boss, to the overall organization and industry.

0 . . . .1. . . . .2. . . . 3 . . . . 4 . . . .5. . . . .6. . . . 7 . . . . 8 . . . .9. . . . 10

2b. When you think about your success, how important is the overall ORGANIZATION? **Check one box.**

☐ Very Important
☐ Somewhat Important
☐ Not Very Important

3a. How closely does your current FINANCIAL COMPENSATION PACKAGE match what you are ideally looking for in a financial compensation package? Financial compensation includes everything from salary, to bonuses, to 401k matching, to vacation time and medical benefits.

0 . . . .1. . . . .2. . . . 3 . . . . 4 . . . .5. . . . .6. . . . 7 . . . . 8 . . . .9. . . . 10

3b. When you think about your success, how important is your FINANCIAL COMPENSATION PACKAGE? **Check one box.**

☐ Very Important
☐ Somewhat Important
☐ Not Very Important

4a. How closely do your current PROFESSIONAL REWARDS match what you are ideally looking for in professional rewards? Professional rewards include everything from respect and recognition for your talents, to leadership opportunities, pathways to promotion, intellectual challenge and job stability.

0 . . . . 1 . . . . .2 . . . . 3 . . . . 4 . . . .5 . . . .6 . . . . 7 . . . . 8 . . . .9 10

4b. When you think about your success, how important are your PROFESSIONAL REWARDS? **Check one box.**

☐ Very Important
☐ Somewhat Important
☐ Not Very Important

FOUR COMPONENTS OF SANITY

Introduction: This part of the quiz examines four specific components of sanity.

5a. How closely does the amount of TIME you currently have outside of work match with the amount of time you ideally would like to have? Time includes everything from spending time on relationships as well as time for hobbies, interests and volunteer activities.

0 . . . . 1 . . . . .2 . . . . 3 . . . . 4 . . . .5 . . . .6 . . . . 7 . . . . 8 . . . .9 10

5b. When you think about your sanity, how important is TIME to you?

Check one box.

☐ Very Important
☐ Somewhat Important
☐ Not Very Important

0 = It does not match at all.
10 = It's a complete match.

6a. How closely does the amount of ENERGY you currently have match with the amount of energy you ideally would like to have? Energy includes both mental and physical energy.

0 . . . .1 . . . . .2 . . . . 3 . . . . 4 . . . .5 . . . . .6 . . . . 7 . . . . 8 . . . .9 10

6b. When you think about your sanity, how important is ENERGY to you? **Check one box.**

☐ Very Important
☐ Somewhat Important
☐ Not Very Important

7a. How closely do your current FINANCIAL RESOURCES match with your ideal financial resources? Financial resources include having the money to pay your bills as well as having the financial means to do things you enjoy.

0 . . . .1 . . . . .2 . . . . 3 . . . . 4 . . . .5 . . . . .6 . . . . 7 . . . . 8 . . . .9 10

7b. When you think about your sanity, how important are FINANCIAL RESOURCES to you? **Check one box.**

☐ Very Important
☐ Somewhat Important
☐ Not Very Important

8a. How closely do the RELATIONSHIPS you currently have in your life match the relationships you ideally would like to have? Relationships can include everything from a spouse, to a partner, to children, to friends, to family, to pets.

0 . . . .1 . . . . .2 . . . . 3 . . . . 4 . . . .5 . . . . .6 . . . . 7 . . . . 8 . . . .9 10

8b. When you think about your sanity, how important are RELATIONSHIPS to you? **Check one box.**

☐ Very Important
☐ Somewhat Important
☐ Not Very Important

EVALUATION OF YOUR SUCCESS & SANITY

To interpret your answers from the previous pages, it's important to look at where you have significant gaps in where you *are* compared to what you *want* (points of pain) and where you have high scores on components that are very important to you (areas of advantage).

POINTS OF PAIN

Points of pain occur when something that is very important to you is not going well. They are the areas of biggest disconnect between what you want, and what you have. Since points of pain tend to cause women significant stress, they should be among the first areas to focus on in any coaching program.

AREAS OF ADVANTAGE

Areas of advantage occur when something that is important to you is going well. They are the areas of greatest consistency between what you want and what you have. These are the areas of surplus for you and you should celebrate them, enjoy them, nurture them and leverage them.

EVALUATION GRID

Use the table below to list the components of both Success and Sanity that you checked as Very Important on Part II of this quiz. Next, record your score for each component that you've listed. Finally, evaluate whether the component is causing you PAIN, providing you an ADVANTAGE, or is NEUTRAL based on the following scoring:

0-4 = PAIN   5-7 = NEUTRAL   8-10 = ADVANTAGE

Very Important Component	Score	Pain, Neutral, Advantage
Example: Professional Rewards	4	Pain

REVIEWING YOUR RESULTS

If you have Points of Pain and/or Areas of Advantage, they probably do not come as a great surprise to you. Most women are intuitively aware of things that are going well or not well in their lives even if they are not able to articulate the details. The evaluation grid is specifically designed to help you identify and articulate the details.

Take some time to reflect on your responses in the grid. Notice your Points of Pain and your Areas of Advantage. Take pride in your Areas of Advantage, but pay close attention to your Points of Pain.

Points of Pain are the things that are not going well for you. They represent your unmet goals, your areas of stress, and your sources of frustration. As such, it's important to address your Points of Pain right away.

TAKING ACTION

After reflection, it's time to take action. Your initial piece of action is to determine which of your Points of Pain to tackle first (if you have more than one on your grid).

You can either choose the one that is most important to you or the one you believe you can make the quickest progress on. There are merits to both approaches, so go with the one that feels right to you.

Next, make a list of concrete actions you can take to address this particular point of pain. If it's ENERGY you lack– look to resources on healthy eating, exercise, and proper sleep. If it's your FINANCIAL COMPENSATION that causes you the greatest pain, look for promotional opportunities within your organization that offer greater financial compensation. If you are not currently qualified for those positions, gain additional education or training that gets you better qualified.

The list of actions to take is endless. Reach out to mentors for advice and support, utilize the internet for expert opinions and additional resources, and refer to specific topics in this book for help.

Review your list daily. Commit to reducing your Points of Pain as a top priority. Evaluate your point of pain weekly and track your progress. Celebrate incremental victories even if they do not meet your overall goals.

What are your overall goals? What should they be? Is it enough to improve your score from a 2 to a 4, or should your goals be more ambitious than that?

Only you will know how much progress it takes to alleviate the stress and frustration that Points of Pain cause you. However, I generally recommend that your goal be to move all Points of Pain to a minimum of a neutral status. This will take time. Be patient, yet persistent.

Points of Pain	Neutral	Areas of Advantage
Scores of 0 - 4	Scores of 5 - 7	Scores of 8 - 10
↑	↑	
If you are here	Make this your goal.	

MOVING FORWARD

Information is power and this chapter has empowered you with specific information about your success and sanity. You have identified the gaps between what you have and what you want overall, and you have identified specific areas of surplus and unmet goals. Armed with that information, you can begin to create a plan for achieving your personal and your professional goals.

If you find that your results do not resonate with you, try taking the quiz again on another day. Sometimes certain events can cause people to answer questions in a knee-jerk reaction that does not reflect their true feelings. It's important that your results reflect your honest and true feelings.

Goals, unlike personality traits, do fluctuate over time, so plan on revisiting this quiz every few months as a way of re-evaluating your success and sanity. Remember to use your results as a way of steering you toward the chapters in this book most relevant to you. Many busy working women do not have the time to read a book from start to finish and I can appreciate that. I designed the chapters to be read in whatever order best meets your needs.

With that said, you won't want to skip the next chapter. It's a quick read and is applicable to all working women who seek greater sanity in their lives. It reveals three simple steps to implement secrets that many women have found helpful.

chapter

Three Simple Secrets That Will Change Your Life

If you read nothing else, read this chapter.

I got a phone call late one afternoon from my friend Michelle*. She was calling on her way home from work. "I've only got five minutes before I pull into my driveway, and I need your help!" she said.

Michelle wanted to know if I could recommend a good book that would help her regain sanity in her life. She felt as though she was barely holding it all together. Despite a loving husband who was her equal partner in parenting, she felt overwhelmed and under-prepared for her roles as mother and career woman. She was hoping I knew of a book that could help.

* Names and other personal information about the people discussed in the book have been changed as requested.

Even if my own book had been ready at the time, I suspected that she would not have time to read it. Women who crave information the most are often the ones with the least amount of time to digest it. I could tell by the tone in her voice that she needed something more tangible than a pep talk. She needed strategies that she could implement right away.

My brain switched into high gear and I quickly came up with the three most effective strategies I've used over the years to manage my own sanity. If you have only five minutes to read anything in this book, read these three proven strategies. They are not only for working mothers with small children, but are applicable for all professional women.

THREE SIMPLE SECRETS

1 **Set limits on your time.** Do not let a project dictate how much time you spend on it.

2 **Carve out catch-up time.** Both your work and your personal life need it.

3 **Reassess your expectations.** You can't be all things to all people all of the time.

SECRET #1: SET LIMITS ON YOUR TIME

Setting the amount of time you spend on any particular project is one of the hardest but most effective strategies for a working woman's sanity. The projects at work obey the gas laws of chemistry – they will fill the time and space you give them.

Therefore, the simple strategy is to limit the time and space that you give any project. Take for example a performance review. In a time-limitless world, you might spend 2-4 hours on a single performance review. You would work on it until you felt like it was done right, no matter how much time that required. Your sanity would take a back seat to the well-thought out and articulate review your employee deserved.

Guess what? Spending more time on a project does not guarantee a better outcome. We just think that it does. We feel guilty putting time constraints on our work. Get over the guilt. Sanity requires discipline, and your discipline must be making tough decisions about how to allocate your time.

A common mistake most people make is confusing the amount of time we spend on a task with what kind of employee we are. Better employees spend more time on projects, right? Not necessarily. Do not confuse time spent on an assignment with the quality of your performance. Reduction in time spent does not equal reduction in quality of performance. Reward yourself, rather than punish yourself, for your efficiency.

If you believe a project requires at least two hours of your time in order to get it done right, challenge yourself to finish it in 60 to 90 minutes. Pretend that you only have exactly that amount of time to get it out the door. Force yourself to finish it in the time that you've allotted. In the past, you probably only finished half the project in 60 or 90 minutes, so you had no choice but to spend more time on it just to have a finished product.

In this new version of time management, you have a completely finished product in less time and you can choose to go back and make changes to it if time allows. The goal in setting limits on your time is to at least produce a finished product in the allotted time. Don't let the project dictate how much time you spend, YOU dictate how much time you're going to spend. It's active versus passive time management.

What you will find over time, as you practice this strategy, is that you minds gets used to the time constraints and actually thinks more clearly because it knows it's on a limited timeframe. The mind that has no time limits set on it tends to wander and be less focused.

I discovered this strategy by necessity after the birth of my first child. Her daycare closed at 5:30pm and that did not mean 5:31pm. There were no late fees at the daycare to help alleviate the guilt of arriving after 5:30pm - only the exhausted faces of the daycare providers who waited patiently for your arrival.

Because this was our first choice in childcare centers, we made adjustments in our work schedule to accommodate the pick-up time. The biggest adjustment was my need to stop whatever I was doing by 5:00pm, so that I could be en route to daycare by 5:15pm. As a person who routinely worked until 6:30 or 7:00pm before having a child, it was a big adjustment.

What I discovered in my new schedule is that my mind got really sharp around 3:00pm each afternoon, in anticipation of projects that needed to be completed before the end of the day. In the past, I had a whole night ahead to finish a project if I needed it. Now I had a little over two hours to finish up whatever needed to be done that day. My mind mentally set the timer for two hours, and I went into overdrive to finish up necessary projects.

Setting such a timer requires you to have discipline, but you will feel the rewards immediately and the rewards will keep you coming back to this strategy again and again.

SECRET #2: CARVE OUT CATCH-UP TIME

Setting limits on your time is a very effective strategy, but what happens when you start to fall behind? What happens when the piles on your desk keep getting taller no matter how many time limits you set for yourself? What you need is a time buffer to fall back on. This buffer is what I call catch-up time.

For many years, catch-up time has been my #1 strategy for sanity and success. The strategy started long before I was a working mom or even a working woman. It started when I was in college. I used to spend Friday nights studying at the library while most of my friends were out having fun. For me, getting caught up was fun because it gave me sanity. I felt calm and self-righteous on Saturday when my friends were just beginning to think about their homework, and I was well on my way to finishing mine.

My secret catch-up time stayed with me when I became a working professional. I carved out time at the office when no one else or very few people were there - usually Monday nights and late Sunday afternoons. I was able to squeeze in an additional 8-10 hours a week of uninterrupted work time. I'm a night owl by nature, so I especially enjoyed my Monday nights, sometimes working well past midnight. The key to catch-up time is finding productive, predictable time that works well for you.

How is catch-up time any different from routinely working a 10-hour day or squeezing in a few extra hours here or there when you can? There are two important differences:

- Catch-up time is predictable, scheduled, and routine. It needs to be uninterrupted time you can count on each week, not just time that might happen.

- Catch-up time needs to happen outside of the normal business hours, so that you are not interrupted by phone calls, meetings or the well-intentioned chit chat in the hallways.

Catch-up time is golden. You will find that each hour of catch-up time is as productive as about two hours of normal work time, because it's free of interruptions.

Catch-up time may seem burdensome or unrealistic at first, but I challenge you to give it a try. It's amazing what you can accomplish in a few hours if you are concurrently employing Secret #1 and Secret #2.

By having scheduled catch-up time each week, I was able to leave the office for daycare pickup without needing to bring work home with me on most nights. I believe that the separation of work and home is essential to your sanity, so it's important that you don't turn your home into an extension of your office. Catch-up time at the office gives you a strategy to get your work done while maintaining the separation between work and home.

Catch-up time is important for your personal life, too.Catch-up time started off strictly as a work strategy for me, but later evolved into a strategy for maintaining my personal relationships as well. I discovered that relationships were not all that different than work. They needed scheduled and predictable catch-up time, too. So, my husband and I implemented a catch-up night that we call date night. Date night has been every other Thursday night for the past five years.

Why Thursday night? That was the closest thing to a weekend night that our babysitter was willing to commit to on a regular basis. Remember, date night like catch-up night needs to be something that is scheduled and routine. You can't just hope it might happen.

Date night is an indulgent expense, but twice a month I can count on dinner and adult conversation with my husband without the kids interrupting us. It's hard to put a price tag on that.

SECRET #3: REASSESS YOUR EXPECTATIONS

This last secret is less tactical than the first two, but equally as important to managing your overall sanity. It's about reassessing your expectations. The difficult pill for most working women to swallow is that the expectations we have of ourselves are largely self-imposed. We want to be all things to all people all the time and anything less feels like failure. Being super-human takes a lot of energy that zaps your success and your sanity. Are you the type of woman who expects herself to be superhuman? If so, why? Are your expectations externally or internally imposed?

When it comes to your performance at work, your boss's expectations are probably the most relevant to you. So what are your boss's expectations? Are you able to meet those expectations (which in many cases are less than the expectations you have of yourself). If you are able to meet them, then you need to let go of your own expectations and re-adjust. If you are not able to meet them, then you need to re-assess your ability to find success and sanity in your current job.

If you are like my friend Michelle and have young children, it is almost impossible to spend the same amount of time at work after you become a mom than you did before you became a mom.

Having children is like taking a crash course in how to multi-task. It's total immersion multi-tasking by necessity. Chances are you are even more efficient at work than you were before you had children. Your brain has a very strong incentive to work smarter, not harder, because it has to.

To give work less time does not mean you love it any less, just like a mother does not love her first born child any less when a second child comes along. You can love your work and your family. Women have an amazing capacity to love a lot of things. It's not "all or nothing" when it comes to work and family. Don't make it a contest when it doesn't have to be one.

Do not beat yourself up about re-assessing your expectations. You don't need or deserve the additional guilt. What you could expect of yourself at a different point in your life may not be what you can expect of yourself right now. Expectations are not set in stone. Re-assess them from time to time as the circumstances in your life change.

PERMISSION TO PUT THIS BOOK DOWN NOW

Books are a great tool and I hope you have time to read this one in its entirety. But if you don't, put the book down right now and begin implementing these three simple strategies in your life. You'll be amazed at the immediate impact they will have on your sanity.

chapter

Five Fundamental
Truths About Business

In my experience, there are five fundamental truths in business that are absolutely essential for success no matter who you are. These five truths were carved into stone long before you or I entered the business world and will be around long after we leave.

These principles are the basic rules of business, and they are as important to your career success as any business class you took in college or graduate school.

You should consider these truths to be universal. They apply to East Coast companies, West Coast companies, and all the companies in between. They apply to big business, small business, publicly and privately held business. They apply to start-up companies and age-old companies. They apply to all employees – male and female alike.

I am certain that most of you will nod your head in agreement as you read the truths listed below. As obvious as they might seem, don't dismiss them. Think about them, absorb them. I know there are a few of you that will feel the need to take exception with them because that's just what some of you like to do. I suggest you save your energy for debating other ideas presented throughout the book that are arguably more opinion than fact. These five fundamental truths are fact.

As you read each truth, ask yourself how often you adhere to it in your daily activities at work. Under what circumstances do you or would you consider violating it? If you have violated one, what have been the consequences or the rewards? Sad but true, some organizations actually reward bad behavior. Do the leaders within you organization adhere to these truths as well?

TRUTH #1
INTEGRITY IS EVERYTHING.

Are you an honest, decent and trustworthy person? Do you act with the highest level of integrity in the workplace?

If you have any doubt as to whether you are acting honorably at work take the Grandma Test. It's a test of basic integrity. First, think of a person you admire and respect who is fairly removed from your current work environment.

Next, take time to talk to that person about your work and see how she responds.

That person for me was my Grandma Lucy (thus the name the Grandma Test). She lived to be 95 years old and was fortunate to have a sharp mind her entire life. I talked with her every Sunday afternoon for the last 15 years of her life – a timeframe that coincided with my years in the corporate world.

I often talked to my Grandma about what was happening at work because I knew she'd push back and ask questions about things that my corporate friends and I took for granted. My talks with Grandma Lucy became my weekly test of integrity.

Could I explain to Grandma Lucy's satisfaction the need for the most recent round of layoffs at work? Could I explain to her why I got a sizable year-end bonus when equally hard-working individuals did not? Could I explain to her why we chose not to tell a client about a mistake we made when we could correct it without them ever knowing?

If you believe the important person in your life would support your actions and your decisions, then you pass the Grandma Test. If you do not, you need to re-evaluate your integrity. At the end of the day, you need to answer to your own conscious, not the conscious of your boss or your boss's boss. It's important to be a good corporate soldier, but never at the expense of selling your soul to the highest bidder.

Bottom Line: Your integrity is not up for sale. Do not shop it to the highest bidder. Take the Grandma Test regularly and make sure you're not getting caught up in a corporate culture that requires or permits diminished integrity.

TRUTH #2
CONFIDENTIALITY IS KEY.

If you can't keep a secret, you can't be an effective leader. Your ability to keep things confidential is paramount to your success. Answer the following question to find out just how leak-proof your lips really are.

Scenario: You are invited to a private meeting with other leaders within your organization and you are informed by the CEO that the company is going to have some sweeping layoffs in the weeks ahead. You are told to keep the information strictly confidential until further notice. Do you:

A. Tell no one. I mean no one.

B. Tell no one except your spouse, but only if you can trust that he'd sooner forget your birthday than leak your secret.

C. Tell no one directly, but hint to others. You are keeping your word by not really telling others, but it's just too hard to keep such a big secret to yourself.

D. Share the information with your closest confidants under strict orders that they tell no one. You want to prepare them for what could be impacting them or their departments. You know you can trust that they will keep the information secret.

E. Slowly leak the information to others in your department because you know that other people from the meeting will leak the information as well and you don't want your department to be the last to know.

F. Tell no one until you start hearing other people within the organization talk about it openly. At that point you feel it's necessary to disclose that you are aware of the information. You hope that by confirming it, you can start calming people down and stop the rumors from getting any worse.

G. Blatantly disregard the mandate for silence and tell the people that you think should know, but ask them to keep it quiet until the news goes public.

If you answered anything other than A or B, you are honest but not leak- proof. The other answers may seem justifiable to you under certain circumstances, but they are not. When you are told to keep information in confidence, it means to tell no one, to hint to no one.

You need to be able to look directly in the eye of anyone who asks you if you know about the information and say you do not. There is nothing more detrimental to your career advancement than being known as the person who can't keep a secret. Believe me, everyone knows who these people are and you don't want to be one of them.

Bottom Line: Be trusted to keep things confidential. Leaking a secret feels good for a moment because it confirms the power that you have (knowledge is power), but the long-term consequences are not worth it.

TRUTH #3

YOUR POSITIVE TRAITS MUST OUTWEIGH YOUR NEGATIVE ONES.

Let's face it, no one is perfect. We all have bad traits. In the end, your positive traits must outweigh your negative ones. People must be able to count on you for the consistency of your good traits as much as they can count on the consistency of your bad traits.

Put yourself in the shoes of your biggest fan at work and answer the following questions:

A. List something that (insert your name) does at work that brings out the best in her.

B. Can you count on her to consistently do this same good thing over and over again under a variety of different circumstances?

Now put yourself in the shoes of your harshest critic at work and answer the following questions:

A. List something that (insert your name) does at work that does not put her at the top of her game?

B. Does she repeat this same shortcoming over and over again under a variety of different circumstances?

Repeat this exercise until you run out of both positive and negative things to say about yourself. Did you have many more positive things to say than negative things? If so, you are on a successful career path.

Your goal is to off-set your consistently bad traits with consistently good ones. People will be willing to forgive and overlook your consistently negative qualities if they are balanced with consistently positive qualities in return.

Bottom line: Your co-workers have good memories. They will remember both the positive and the negative things that you repeatedly do.

TRUTH #4
NEVER LET YOUR BOSS BE BLINDSIDED.
YOUR JOB IS TO MAKE YOUR BOSS LOOK GOOD.

You answer your phone late one afternoon and your very unhappy boss is screaming on the other end, "Why didn't you tell me that account was in jeopardy? Why didn't you tell me that the client was going to call my boss directly complaining about our services? Why did you let me get blindsided?"

Your boss is angry with you because she was embarrassed in front of her boss. She had no idea that things were going wrong on the account because you had not been keeping her informed of any problems. You thought that by keeping the problems quiet, and trying to handle them yourself, you were doing your boss a favor. You were dead wrong.

If this situation sounds at all familiar, you have committed one of the cardinal sins in corporate America – *Thou shall not let your boss be blindsided.* Your job is to make your boss look good. Your boss can not look good if she gets blindsided.

Part of being a great employee is being a great information filter. How and when you keep your boss informed of important information is an art and not a science. This is an important skill to hone throughout your career.

You don't want to be Chicken Little telling your boss every time the sky is falling when little things go wrong. Your boss will stop listening to you.

On the other hand, if you keep too many things from her, you run the risk of letting her hear about important information from someone other than you. You don't want that to happen. In the end, you need to have keen discretion in predicting what might get escalated to your boss or your boss's boss and make sure you get that information to your boss first.

Some organizations have a culture that thrives on escalation which means that people are given credit for being an alarmist and escalating potential problems outside of the normal chain of command. How do you know if you're in one of those organizations? A tell-tale sign is if you see e-mails going out to you and your boss or other high ranking officials all at the same time.

The goal here is to give you no chance to problem solve prior to notifying your boss. There is no real reason for this practice to occur, but in some organizations, people are rewarded for escalating information and in such cases, blindsiding becomes the name of the game. If you are in

Types of Information to Be Shared with a Boss

As an employee, I categorize information I pass onto my boss in three distinct buckets.

Must Know Now

The first bucket is reserved for very critical information that your boss needs to know right away. Don't send this type of information in an e-mail unless that is your very last resort.

Make sure that when you are delivering critical information in person that it really is critical. Bosses quickly learn who exaggerates and who does not. You lose credibility when you are labeled as the exaggerator.

Need to Know

The second bucket typically means something that requires action or judgment on your boss's part, but not immediately. If your boss likes e-mail, you can send "Need to know" information via e-mail in a daily or weekly report.

Nice To Know

The third bucket can best be thought of as an FYI (For Your Information). It's information that needs no action or attention by your boss. Some bosses do not even want to receive "Nice to know" information. Find out from your boss what his/her preferences are.

one of these organizations, you need to make sure you don't let your boss get blindsided.

How much information your boss wants to receive is a very personal thing, and there is no equation for what is right or wrong. In time you will learn what her threshold is. It's best to err on the side of too much information until your boss makes it clear that less information is preferable.

Bottom Line: Have a plan in place to actively gather and filter information for your boss so that she is neither overwhelmed with minutiae nor blindsided by something important. Ask your boss what level of information she wants to receive from you and how she prefers to receive it.

TRUTH #5
COMPANIES HAVE FINANCIAL RESPONSIBILITIES.

If you can feel your skin crawl when you hear words like profit, return on investment, shareholders, and bottom line, then Corporate America may not be the right place for you. There is no way around the fact that making money for the investors is a primary responsibility of for-profit companies. As a paid member of one of these companies, you need to care about making money, too. When all goes well, for-profit companies can make money *and* have a great corporate culture. It's not an either/or situation.

In fact, companies that can do both are the companies that you want to find and be a part of. Companies with a great corporate culture who can't make money are typically not sustainable. So if you're part of one of these companies, enjoy the great ride while it lasts, but make sure your resume is up to date.

As a responsible employee in a for-profit company, you need to take an interest in your company's financials and be aware of how your company is doing. Take ownership of the financial situation, regardless of your position within the organization. Familiarize yourself with whatever financial information is made available to you. Research shows that profit and loss (P&L) experience is one of the most important factors in job promotion, yet women greatly lack this experience (*Catalyst*, 2008).

It's never too late to learn, so don't worry if you were not an accounting major, or if you never even took an accounting class in college. I didn't take one either, and I'm living proof that even a non-business major can gain P&L experience.

Familiarize yourself with corporate financials and ask for small P&L responsibility to start with. Demonstrate a firm understanding of your company's financials in everything you do from cost-containment, to up-sell opportunities, to speed-to-market on new products. Make all your decisions with your company's financials in mind.

Bottom Line: P&L experience and financial knowledge are key contributors to upper level corporate promotions.

Find a way to get this experience if those are the positions you desire.

At the end of the day, if you simply can not embrace the importance of income, expenses and profit margins, then consider work outside of for-profit corporations. Remember though, almost no organization, even a not-for-profit, works on an unlimited budget.

Cost-containment and financial accountability are going to be part of your life almost anywhere you go. Embrace them or avoid them? I suggest you embrace them without ever losing sight of Truth #1: Integrity is Everything.

chapter

Making Smart Career Choices: A Reality Check

No matter where you are in your career, it's never too early or too late to make smart career choices. A smart career choice begins with a reality check – it's an honest and realistic evaluation of where you are now in your career and, more importantly, where you want to be 2-3 years from now.

Long-range career planning (5+ years) is important too, but the truth is that what you do in the next 2-3 years will determine what opportunities you have later on. So, planning too far down the road is not fruitful if you are unable to meet your 2-3 year career goals.

Making smart choices involves looking at your life as a total picture. How do your career goals fit in with the rest of your life? Do you see a coherent picture or a tangled mess? Smart career choices are about setting professional goals that authentically and honestly blend with the reality of your life as it stands today – not as you ideally want it to be.

Your ability to make smart career choices is partially based on your knowledge of what employers' value most in their employees. Each employer is different, but this chapter highlights seven dimensions that have universal appeal to most corporate employers.

The exercise below is a brief reality check. It's not an all inclusive career planning guide, but it will help you realize what areas of your life are consistent and inconsistent with your career goals. It will help you see where your strengths and weaknesses are through the eyes of an employer, so that you are better prepared to make smart career choices for yourself.

Note: Not all professional careers have traditional management tracks similar to those in the corporate world. Women who are in academics, medicine, law or other technical fields should be advised that this reality-check exercise is based on my corporate experiences. I do not know how it will translate to your profession.

Seven dimensions of you as an employee

1. My Education

2. My Work Experience

3. My Family Commitments

4. My Additional Commitments

5. My Ability to Travel

6. My Promotional History

7. My Ability to Relocate

REALITY CHECK EXERCISE

Directions: Read each statement beneath the dimensions listed below and check the statement that most closely matches your life – not as you want it to be, but as it is. Complete the quiz first before looking at the scoring that begins on page 71.

1. My Education   Score ☐

☐   I have about the same education as other people seeking the same positions that I'm seeking.

☐   I have an additional degree that will differentiate me from other people seeking the same positions that I'm seeking.

2. My Work Experience   Score ☐

☐   I am still early in my professional career and do not have a lot of significant experience yet.

☐   I have significant professional experience in my chosen field. I am not in a management position.

☐   I have significant professional experience in my chosen field. I am in a management position (manager or director).

☐   I have significant professional experience in my chosen field. I am in an upper management position (Vice President or higher).

☐   I am moving into the later phase of my career. I have less than 5 years before retirement.

3. My Family Commitments Score ☐

- ☐ I have few significant family commitments that I need to coordinate with my work.

- ☐ I have some significant family commitments that I need to coordinate with work, but I get alot of help in meeting those commitments.

- ☐ I have some significant family commitments that I need to coordinate with work, and I get some help in meeting those commitments.

- ☐ I have a full plate of family commitments and I get little help in managing them.

4. My Additional Commitments Score ☐

- ☐ I do not have any significant social or community involvement outside of work that demands my time.

- ☐ I participate in some community involvement outside of work.

- ☐ I am very actively involved in community activities outside of work that place significant demands on my time (school, local politics, religious involvement, community theater, sports, charitable organizations, etc.).

5. My Ability to Travel Score ☐

- ☐ Business travel does not complicate my life. I have no problem doing it.

- ☐ Business travel does complicate my life, but I am willing to do as much of it as is required for my job.

☐ Business travel complicates my life and I would prefer a job that has limited travel (one trip or less a month).

☐ My ideal job would have little or no travel requirements.

6. My Promotional History   Score ☐

☐ I am new to my current organization.

☐ I have been with my current organization less than 2 years and have not been promoted, but I have received favorable performance reviews.

☐ I have been promoted once within my current organization.

☐ I have been promoted more than once within my current organization.

☐ I have been with my current organization 2-5 years and have not been promoted.

☐ I have been with my current organization more than 5 years and have not been promoted.

7. My Ability to Relocate   Score ☐

☐ I am unable to relocate.

☐ I am open to the idea of relocation.

☐ I am completely able to relocation.

SCORING

STEP 1:

Go back and record your points in the boxes to the right of each dimension based on the following scoring.

1. My Education

- I have about the same education as other people seeking the same positions that I'm seeking. **Score 0 points**

- I have an additional degree that will differentiate me from other people seeking the same positions that I'm seeking. **Score 2 points**

2. My Work Experience

- I am still early in my professional career and do not have a lot of significant experience yet. **Score 0 point.**

- I have significant professional experience in my chosen field. I am not in a management position. **Score 1 point**

- I have significant professional experience in my chosen field. I am in management position (manager or director). **Score 2 points.**

- I have significant professional experience in my chosen field. I am in an upper management position (Vice President or higher). **Score 3 points.**

- I am moving into the latter phases of my career. I have less than 5 years before retirement. **Score 0 point**

3. My Family Commitments

- I have little to no significant family commitments that I need to coordinate with my work. **Score 3 points**

- I have some significant family commitments that I need to coordinate with work but I get a lot of help in meeting those commitments. **Score 2 points**

- I have some significant family commitments that I need to coordinate with work, and I get some help in meeting those commitments. **Score 1 point**

- My plate of family commitments is completely full right now and I get little help in managing them. **Score 0 points**

4. My Additional Commitments

- I do not have any significant social or community involvement outside of work that demands my time. **Score 2 points**

- I participate in some community involvement outside of work but not a lot. **Score 1 point**

- I am very actively involved in community activities outside of work that place significant demands on my time (school, local politics, religious involvement, community theater, sports, charitable organizations, etc.). **Score 0 points**

5. My Ability to Travel

- Business travel does not complicate my life. I have no problem doing it. **Score 2 points**

- Business travel does complicate my life, but I am willing to do as much of it as is required for my job. **Score 2 points**

- Business travel complicates my life and I would prefer a job that has limited travel (1 trip or less a month). Score **1 point**

- My ideal job would have little or no travel requirements. **Score 0 points**

6. My Promotional History

- I am new to my current organization. **Score 0 points**

- I have been with my current organization less than 2 years and have not been promoted yet, but have received favorable performance reviews. **Score 1 point**

- I have been promoted once within my current organization. **Score 2 point**

- I have been promoted more than once within my current organization. **Score 3 points**

- I have been with my current organization 2-5 years and have not been promoted yet. **Score 0 points**

- I have been with my current organization more than 5 years and have not been promoted yet. **Subtract 1 point.**

7. My Ability to Relocate

- I am unable to relocate. **Score 0 points**

- I am open to the idea of relocation. **Score 1 point**

- I am completely able to relocation. **Score 2 points**

STEP 2:

Check the response below that most closely matches your goals over the next 2-3 years.

My 2-3 Year Goal:

☐ a. My 2-3 year goal does not include being in a management position.

☐ b. My 2-3 year goal is to be in lower management. (Supervisor, Manager)

☐ c. My 2-3 year goal is to be in middle management (Director, Executive Director)

☐ d. My 2-3 year goal is to be in upper management. (Vice President, Senior Vice President)

☐ e. My 2-3 year career goal is to be in a top management position (Chief Operating Officer (COO), Chief Financial Officer (CFO), Chief Technology Officer (CTO), Chief Executive Officer (CEO), and Presidents)

HOW CLOSE ARE YOU TO YOUR GOALS?

The point requirements listed below are based on my experience with levels of management in corporate America. You may need to make adjustments according to your organization's particular management structure and use of titles.

Point Requirements

a. If your goal is to be in a top management position (CFO, CTO, COO, President, and CEO), you'll need *15 or more points.*

> *You are aiming big and it will take the right combination of skills, lifestyle situation, determination, and good fortune to get where you want to go. Go for it!*

b. If your goal is to be in upper management, (Vice President or SVP), you'll need *11 to 14 points.*

c. If your goal is to be in middle management, (Director, Executive Director), you'll need *6 to 10 points.*

d. If your goal is to be in lower management, (Supervisor, Manager), you'll need *3 to 5 points.*

e. If you're not looking to be in a management position, then n*o particular number of points required. This does not mean you can get lazy on the job. Job performance is still important for your job security even if management is not in your 2-3 year career goals.*

Did your score match up with your goals? If not, don't lose hope yet. It's possible that your goals are simply too far out of line to be attainable in the next 2-3 years. However, it's also possible that your goals are within reach if you are able to make certain changes in your life.

Read the following descriptions for each dimension to learn more about why that dimension is important and what it takes to get the most points.

The reality is that management positions come with certain expectations. The higher you are in management, the greater the expectations.

If you are not in a position to meet those expectations at this time, are you in a position to make the changes you need to meet those expectations in the future?

THE IMPORTANCE OF THESE 7 DIMENSIONS

What is so important about these dimensions? Why do they matter? As I stated previously, meeting your 2-3 year career goals lays the foundation for meeting your longer-term career goals. Each of these dimensions plays a key part in your ability to meet your 2-3 year goals.

1. Education

Your education matters the most when you are seeking your first professional job and again when you are seeking subsequent management or senior-level jobs. You might think that the importance of education should give way to the importance of experience as you advance in your career, and to some extent it does - especially when you are advancing your career within the same company.

However, the importance of education never completely fades away because education is an integral part of your resume and new employers use resumes as part of their hiring process. So, your education lives on through your resume for your entire career. Anytime someone reviews your resume, they are judging your education.

Not surprisingly, it's not actually how you did in school that matters most on your resume. It's what degrees you earned and where you went to school. This does not mean that you should not indicate graduating with honors or various named distinctions if you have them, because you should. It just means that it's the degree itself as much as your performance at the school that impresses most potential employers.

For the sake of scoring this dimension, you got a zero if you have about the same education as other candidates, because you do not differentiate yourself from others on this dimension. If you have an advanced degree that is "preferred" but "not required" for the job, you earn leverage on this dimension and thus score a 2. Education is important and it's an all or nothing (you can't really have half a degree), thus the scoring of 0 or 2.

2. Work Experience

Work experience is one of the most significant factors in determining your ability to meet your career goals.

Simply stated, it's because work experience does not typically make exponential leaps. You are unlikely to go from a non-management position to CEO in a short period of time.

Work experience is important because there are logical times when the windows of opportunity open up to people. It does not happen too early in your career and it does not happen too late.

If you reach the mid-point of your career (mid-40s for example) and have not yet had experience managing people, it's less likely that opportunity will come your way in the future.

Major career changes can happen for people later in life if they have gone back to school for additional education or have made other significant changes in their marketability.

However, the majority of experiences that impact career goals start to happen when you are not too early and not too late in your career – like a bell shaped curve.

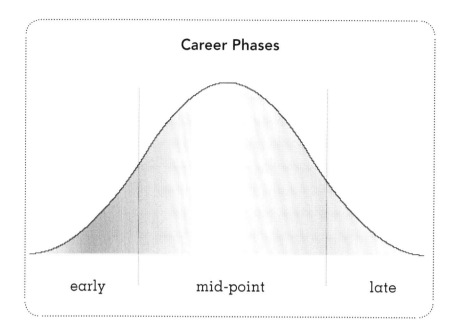

Career Phases

early | mid-point | late

Thus the highest score (score of 3) goes to women in the middle of that curve who have 5-10 years experience and are in management positions.

3. Family Commitments

Family commitments are the area in which success and sanity most closely intersect. It's the area in which the reality of your life comes face to face with the reality of your career choices.

As I stated earlier, women can have it all, we just need to be realistic about defining what having it all means.

To my good friend Nikki, having it all means being a Vice President of a company while having three children currently under the age of seven. She logged 60 business trips last year and still finds time to make homemade candy for her friends at Christmas time. Nikki does not do it all alone. She has a very supportive husband, Tony, whose own job does not have the same time and travel demands that Nikki's does. Tony is very involved in his children's daily lives. Nikki is a testament to the fact that family commitments do not have to limit your success, but they play a significant factor in your career choices.

Points for this dimension simply reflect the amount of time and energy that your family commitments require of you - the greater the demands and the fewer easily available resources to help you with those demands, the fewer the points.

4. Additional Commitments

Harvard Business Review reported research that shows companies would benefit from capitalizing on leadership skills within the workplace that are gained from community involvement outside the workplace (especially among African American women). Therefore, a more progressive scoring would give the most points to the person with the well-rounded outside commitments.

However, most companies still view these outside commitments as a time-constraint that interferes with your ability to be totally available to your company. As a result, the scoring in this section is based on how most organizations view outside commitments today, not as an enlightened company should view them.

5. Ability to Travel

Most careers today require some level of business travel, and obviously some require more than others. A career in sales has notoriously the highest travel requirements. Wanting to be in sales without wanting to do a lot of travel is like wanting to have your cake and eat it calorie-free.

Overnight business travel typically requires some pre-planning if you have family and/or additional commitments discussed in the dimensions above. The many roles you play outside of work may require backup coverage while you are away.

To some women, this means finding a good kennel or a good friend to take care of their dog. To others, this means finding someone else to host this month's book club meeting, or making sure that there is an emergency contact in place to assist your elderly parent should they need help while you are gone. The spectrum of responsibilities that require backup coverage are as diverse as the women themselves.

The fact that business travel takes some extra work does not mean that women should try to avoid it. Quite the opposite; I think business travel is good for the soul. A night in a hotel with someone else washing your sheets and towels can be very therapeutic. I found that sometimes the only chance I got to exercise, relax, and get to bed early was when I was out of town on a business trip away from the responsibilities of my normal life. Those mental breaks did a lot for my sanity.

My sanity sometimes came at the expense of my husband's sanity as he juggled kids, dogs, and his own demanding work schedule, but we each took turns enjoying an occasional business trip away from the responsibilities at home. Occasional is the operative word here. Business travel can go from pleasure to pain very quickly when the trips start to become too much for you or your family.

Only you can define what too much is, but I'm sure you'll know it when you see it. Women who are not burdened by extensive business travel and/or those women who actually enjoy it, score a 2 on this dimension. Women who enjoy or tolerate limited travel score a 1 and those women who really seek a job without any travel score a 0. Professional success without travel is hard to come by.

If you do not like travel, or your family situation makes travel very difficult for you, then look for professions with low travel requirements. Businesses that specialize in local customers might be the right fit for you. International companies or companies with several regional offices are not a good fit for someone who wishes to be in upper management, but does not want to travel. It's just not a realistic option.

6. Promotional History

Your promotional history is important because past behavior strongly predicts future behavior. If you've been promoted in the past there is a good chance that you'll be promoted again in the future (assuming a continuing strong performance on your part).

If you are new to an organization, you can not expect a promotion in the immediate future. A new organization will need some time to evaluate your performance before they tap you for a promotion. Hopefully, the move to the new organization was part of a promotion in and of itself, so now is your time to prove yourself.

A strong promotional history bodes well for women with high aspiring career goals. Promotions beget promotions. If you've been promoted more than once within your current organization that is a very good sign that your organization has a great deal of confidence in you. If you've been with your organization for more than five years and have not received any type of promotion, it's less likely that you're going to get one (unless your organization has a history of very long, drawn-out career tracks.) This is the general premise that underlies the scoring of this dimension.

7. Ability to Relocate

Remember Nikki the Vice President with the three young children who logged 60 business trips in one year? Nikki's success is living proof of the importance of ability to travel and to relocate. Nikki moved from Utah to Minnesota for a chance to further her career. Three years later, she initiated a move back to Utah in search of greater sanity, living near family when her children were very young.

Five years later, she relocated back to Minnesota to become a Vice President. Her ability and openness to relocation has allowed her to achieve her career goals.

Do you know whether relocation might be required of you as you gain greater success within your current organization? Look around you. Have other people who hold the jobs to which you aspire been required to relocate? Have other people along your similar career path taken temporary assignments (1-3 years) out of the country or overseas?

Sometimes the writing is on the wall for the need to relocate. For example, if you're based in a regional office while all the top executives in your organization are based at the company's headquarters, there is a very real chance that you won't become a top executive without moving to headquarters. Are you based in one location while the majority of your direct reports are based in another? If so, it's very possible that you'll be asked to relocate closer to your direct reports. If you're lucky, relocation will be an option, and not a requirement.

Some women welcome relocation, others tolerate it and some simply are not in a position to do it. Be aware of your own ability to relocate and realize that it may be a factor in your ability to achieve certain long-term career goals.

WHERE DOES THIS LEAVE YOU?

The reality check is just that – a reality check. It can not predict your success or failure. Success takes into account much more than these 7 dimensions. What these 7 dimensions can help you do is understand what is important for success through the eyes of an employer.

The exercise was designed to give you insight into what most companies value and what they expect in their successful employees. Armed with this knowledge you can better position yourself to make smart career choices in your own life.

chapter

The Parable of Phoebe Fish:
The Big Fish Little Pond Effect

Like most parables, the Parable of Phoebe Fish is intended to convey an underlying lesson. The fun in reading this chapter is to let the hidden meaning effortlessly unfold as you enjoy the whimsical story of Phoebe Fish that was co-authored with my very own ten-year-old daughter, Kate.

Take full advantage of the dual nature of the parable. Read the story to a child. Let them enjoy the storyline, while you explore the nature of your own professional motivation.

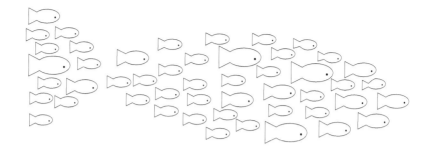

THE STORY

There was nothing particularly special about the day Phoebe Fish arrived in the little pond located at the end of Fieldhouse Way. It was a sunny day with a cool breeze – just enough to make the water sparkle the way it usually did at the surface of the pond.

If there was anything special about that day, it was Phoebe herself. She was one of the biggest fish to ever hatch in Fieldhouse pond. She was not only big, she was bright, too. The brightest blue fish anyone had ever seen. Her fins were large and her scales were shiny. She swam with confidence, just the way big fish do.

Phoebe swam around the pond that day, until she found the other big fish to play with (because being with other big fish is what big fish like to do). Phoebe quickly learned about her many responsibilities in the pond. Big fish were responsible for keeping the pond clean and safe. Big fish were responsible for watching the water levels in the pond, and big fish were responsible for making sure there was enough food for all the little fish.

Big fish were also responsible for teaching the little fish the rules of the pond:

Rule #1 – Get along well with the other fish.

Rule #2 – Do not swim near the surface of the pond where the water is dangerous and choppy. (At least that is the explanation the big fish give the little fish to keep them down near the bottom of the pond.)

Rule #3 – Do not question a big fish's explanations.

Almost every summer, big storms came to Fieldhouse pond. Part of Phoebe's job was to make sure that the little fish were safely protected inside the underwater caverns before the storms hit. Phoebe always knew when a bad storm was coming long before the little fish did. That was part of being a big fish.

In return for all her hard work, Phoebe got to swim at the surface of the water. Only the big fish had that privilege. The surface water was generally warm and sunny and uninterrupted by the splashing of little fish. Sometimes, the water at the surface did get a little choppy, but the big fish had lots of experience in navigating choppy water.

If there is one thing Phoebe loved the most about Fieldhouse pond, it was being at the surface of the water when the farmer came around. The farmer brought oatmeal that he would sprinkle into the water now and again, when he wanted to watch the big fish jump.

He never brought more than a small cup of oatmeal with him (after all, it was a small pond), but the big fish went crazy with delight every time the special treat was sprinkled into the water. The big fish made a contest out of seeing who could get the biggest piece of oatmeal and they carried it around with pride showing it off to the other big fish.

The oatmeal never trickled down far enough to reach the little fish in the lower layers of the pond. Phoebe felt bad about that. She secretly hoped that the little fish did not know about the oatmeal so that she did not have to feel guilty about not sharing it with them.

Life was wonderful at Fieldhouse pond. Phoebe never wanted to leave. Then one day, a truck pulled up next to the pond and a farmer that they'd never seen before came up to the water's edge. He dipped a bucket into the pond and filled it up with fish including Phoebe. He filled several buckets, loaded them onto the back of his truck and drove away.

Phoebe had heard about this from other fish that had been brought into Fieldhouse pond through a similar process. Apparently, farmers did this from time to time when they needed more fish in their ponds – a merger of sorts. From what Phoebe had heard, the fish were generally kept safe on the way to the new pond and only a few fish were not expected to survive the journey.

Phoebe was scared and a little excited as she bounced around in the bucket at the back of the truck. She'd never been away from Fieldhouse pond. What would the new pond look like? Would there be other big fish just like her? Would there be a farmer who brought oatmeal? Her curiosity was never-ending and thankfully the truck finally came to a stop.

One by one, the farmer unloaded the buckets from the truck and dumped them into the new pond. Down, down, down Phoebe fell into unfamiliar water. She seemed to fall deeper and deeper into the water than she'd ever been before. She could tell right away that this pond was much bigger than Fieldhouse pond. She had no idea a pond could be so big. When she finally stopped tumbling downward, she landed in a place that was cold and dark. She was lonely and scared.

"You can do it," she told herself. "You can just turn right around and swim to the surface where the water is sunny and warm. You know your way to the top. You've been there hundreds of times before." So, that is exactly what she began to do. She swam, and she swam, and she swam toward the surface.

Eventually, Phoebe got tired and she stopped to take a little rest. As she was resting, a friendly little fish swam past her. "Hello." said the friendly little fish. "My name is Franny."

Franny was a little fish; a colorful little fish who looked alot like the other little fish around her. There was something special about Franny though that Phoebe liked immediately. Franny was kind, helpful, smart, and sincere.

Phoebe soon learned that Franny had lived in the big pond her entire life and she knew alot about what went on in the big pond. Somewhat to Phoebe's surprise, Franny liked living in the big pond. That knowledge made Phoebe less scared about her new surroundings.

As for Franny, she could not help but stare at Phoebe from the first time they met. She'd seldom been so close to a big fish because big fish did not generally swim with the little fish. Franny was surprised by how much she enjoyed Phoebe's company.

Franny had never been to the surface of the pond and she was fascinated by the stories that Phoebe told her about the warm, sunny water and the oatmeal treats. They spent hours talking and before they knew it, they were best friends.

Franny showed Phoebe all the wonderful things about living in the big pond. There was more room to play, exciting new places to explore, and lots of friendly fish to play with. For a little while, Phoebe forgot how much she missed Fieldhouse pond.

Several nights later, Phoebe experienced her first storm in the big pond. It was so much less scary than the storms at Fieldhouse pond had been because Phoebe was deep down in the calm waters now. She had to admit it was pretty nice to sleep right through a storm rather than staying awake all night bouncing around in the choppy surface waters.

The next morning Phoebe asked Franny, "Don't you ever get tired of not seeing the sunshine?

"No," Franny replied. "When you're a little fish in a big pond, you never see the sun. We can imagine what it might look like, but we don't miss what we've never had.

"It's more peaceful down here," she added. "And, there are lots of great little fish to swim with, too. We don't have to worry about whether the water in the pond is clean and whether there is enough food to go around. We leave those things up to the big fish. Stay here and be a little fish with us!" Franny said to Phoebe.

Phoebe had to admit that the little fish were pretty friendly and less competitive than the big fish she'd known. As much as she hated to admit it, Phoebe looked more like the little fish in the big pond than she cared to accept. Phoebe was not that much bigger than Franny. Phoebe saw herself as a big fish because she'd always been seen by others as a big fish and Franny saw herself as a little fish because she'd always been seen by others as a little fish.

Phoebe realized that she needed to do something extraordinary to get herself noticed by the big fish in the big pond. So, the next day she set out for the surface of the big pond to prove herself to the other big fish. In her heart, she knew she would not be happy until she was back swimming at the surface.

She swam as fast and as hard as she could until she was stopped by a big fish who told her that she was not allowed to swim any closer to the surface. Phoebe had never been stopped on her way to the top and she'd never before seen a fish as big as he was. Even the biggest fish in Fieldhouse pond was small by comparison.

At that exact moment, Phoebe knew what she had to do. She had to get bigger to compete with the big fish in this new pond. Now she was on a mission. She worked night and day getting stronger, faster, and bigger. She did not have as much time to play with Franny anymore.

Eventually, Phoebe did get bigger and she decided it was time to attempt to swim to the surface again. She swam as hard as she could that day, but she did not make it to the surface to see the sunshine. Day after day, Phoebe suffered the same disappointment. She swam as hard as she could toward the surface of the water. She got a glimpse of the sunshine before she was turned away by the big fish who controlled the access to the top.

Phoebe grew increasingly frustrated and she was no longer sure she would like the waters at the top of the big pond, even if she could make it there. She'd seen glimpses of the surface and it did not look as warm and inviting to her as the surface had at Fieldhouse pond. The big fish did not look as friendly in this pond either.

"I wish I could go back to my little pond," she said sadly to Franny one night.

"Is that what you really want?" asked Franny.

"Yes," said Phoebe.

"Then, I'll take you to meet Fletcher" she told Phoebe. "I'm sure he can help you."

"Who is Fletcher?" Phoebe asked.

"Fletcher is a little fish just like me," said Franny. "But he's lived in lots of different ponds. He's been in big ones, little ones, and all sized in between. Fletcher knows about the secret underground streams that connected ponds to each other. If you swim through the streams, you can get to other ponds."

Phoebe had never heard of the underground streams. She knew that some fish were plucked out of the waters by fishing hooks, and some fish were transported by buckets to other ponds like she had been. She'd never heard of a fish actually swimming to a new pond on her own. Her scales tingled with excitement.

"You mean I don't have to stay in this pond forever?" She asked. "You mean I can choose a different pond?"

"Yes," Franny told her.

"Why haven't you gone to a different pond?" Phoebe asked Franny.

"Because I like it here," said Franny. "The water is not always warmer in another pond."

"Why don't more fish know about the secret underground streams?" Phoebe asked. "Why don't more fish use them?"

"The farmers don't want us to know about them," said Franny. "If we knew, we might leave their pond. They want to be the ones to decide if we stay or if we go."

So as promised, the next morning Franny took Phoebe to meet Fletcher. Fletcher agreed to show Phoebe the way to the underground streams.

"Be sure that you really want to go before you swim off," Fletcher warned Phoebe. "It's very difficult, and sometimes impossible, to come back to the same pond once you've left."

Before Phoebe swam away, she tried to convince Franny one more time to come with her. "Little ponds are so beautiful," she told Franny. "You can see from top to bottom and side to side."

"Thanks." said Franny. "But I'm really happy here. I like the calm, cool water. I like knowing that food is plentiful. I like knowing that if there is a drought, the pond will not dry up. I like knowing that there are lots of other fish just like me."

So, Phoebe swam off alone that day in search of a little pond. She knew the right one the minute she saw it. The big fish welcomed Phoebe as one of their own right away. They bestowed on her all the big fish responsibilities and all the big fish favors. She felt at home again.

Phoebe and Franny promised that they would visit each other as often as they could, and they did. Phoebe lived happily ever after as a big fish in a little pond. Franny lived happily ever after as a little fish in a big pond. They never did agree on which pond was actually the best. The one thing they always agreed upon was being best friends.

The End

WHY ALL THE FUSS ABOUT FISH?

The concept in the parable is based on the big-fish-little-pond effect introduced by educational psychologist Dr. Herbert W. Marsh. He did not base his theory on employees per se, but rather on students. He hypothesized that the self-concept of students is negatively correlated with the ability of their student peers. Academic self-concept depends not only on one's own academic accomplishments but also the accomplishments, of those in the school that the student attends.

That explains why a straight-A student who graduates from a small high school feels really smart until she meets students much smarter than she is at her new prestigious college.

By implication, a person's professional self-concept, as defined by her success, depends on the accomplishments of her peers within her organization. Her accomplishments have a greater chance of looking impressive, when she has a smaller group with which to compare them. Simply stated, a person has a better chance of becoming a big fish if she is in a little pond.

It's important to recognize that a person's talents are not absolute. A big fish in a little pond does not automatically remain a big fish when she's moved to a bigger pond. The size of the pond has a direct correlation on the way that your talents are perceived by others.

ASSUMPTIONS

For the sake of the lessons to be learned in the parable, you need to accept the following assumptions:

- All ponds need big fish and little fish in order to survive.

- There are always more little fish than big fish in any pond.

- Big fish generally represent upper management employees and little fish generally represent the non-management employees.

- Big ponds are deeper than little ponds. It takes longer to get from the bottom to the top of the water in a big pond.

- The warm and sunny water at the surface of the pond is where the big fish like to hang out. It represents the top of the organizational chart.

- The single most important factor in determining pond size is revenue – an organization's top line. Big ponds have big revenue, little ponds have smaller revenue.

- A little pond is not inferior to a big pond, just as a little company is not inferior to a big company. There are many superior little ponds and many superior big ponds. The final judgment is up to you.

WHO'S WHO IN THE POND

Phoebe represents a high-aspiring, high-achieving professional woman who identifies herself as a big fish. She is determined to be at the top of the organization, and can not imagine being satisfied with anything less.

Franny represents a loyal employee who finds satisfaction and sanity in the mid-levels of her organization. She clearly identifies herself as a little fish. She is content with the lifestyle that being a little fish in a big pond affords her.

Fletcher represents the mid-level employee who has a strong desire to be in-the-know about what's going on within the organization. Since he's male, he's more likely to be tapped into the underground streams or networks where that kind of information is more readily shared.

The farmer is a composite of people who ultimately have control over the organization – the owners and/or the board of directors. It's not simply by coincidence that the farmer is the only one in the story who never actually gets into the water, but has the final say over what happens to all the fish in the water.

THE POND ITSELF

The pond in the story represents the organization in which you work. The size of a pond is not entirely dependent on the number of people it employs, although that is a factor.

The most significant factor in determining the size of a pond is financial performance. Big ponds generate big revenue and little ponds generate smaller revenue. No other single factor is as important in determining the size of the pond.

With that said, the size of the pond is relative based on your experience and your perspective. A company with $200 million dollars in annual revenue feels big to the person who works for a $20 million dollar company. The same $200 million dollar company feels small to the person who works for a company that generates $2 billion dollars in annual revenue.

During my corporate career, I swam in many different sized ponds and I found that my own success and sanity definitely waxed and waned depending on the size of the pond I was in. My skills did not change significantly, but the way in which my skills were perceived varied as a result of who else was in the pond with me. Big ponds have a larger talent pool and a larger talent pool means more competition for the big fish positions.

Like Phoebe in the story, I prefer being a big fish. I grew up in a small town with one public high school and about 100 people in my graduating class. The small environment allowed me to become a big fish, and I was hooked.

In my professional career, I gravitated toward little ponds where my chances of being a big fish were better. Big fish are not inherently better, but most of us are conditioned by our society to believe that bigger is better. After all, you never hear anglers telling stories about the little fish that got away do you?

WHAT'S THE BIG APPEAL?

What appeals to me about being a big fish? Big fish have power and influence. Big fish are in-the-know. Big fish are at the table for the important events. Big fish have additional responsibilities and more accountabilities that can add up to bigger stress. But to compensate for that, big fish get the big rewards (higher pay, higher bonuses, and better privileges).

The concept of big fish versus little fish begs the question of whether big fish are born or made. There are many educated people who feel very strongly on both sides of this issue. I don't feel strongly about engaging in the debate, although I suspect that it is some combination of natural talent, ambition, opportunity, and societal expectations that propels certain fish to the top of their class.

It is no coincidence and no secret that men reach the top of the pond more often than women. An overwhelming number of studies show that women receive less recognition for their accomplishments than men do. The findings are substantial and consistent.

Women who aspire to be big fish are never going to feel satisfied as a little fish. Success and sanity depend on a close match between a woman's aspirations andher reality.

THE MOST IMPORTANT TAKE-AWAY MESSAGE

There are many different messages that you can take away from this parable, but there is one message that I feel most strongly about. It is this: Every woman has power and influence over her own life, even if she lacks power in the organization that she works for.

As women, we are inherently loyal to our bosses, our teams, and our organizations. In general, I see this as a good thing. However, when we are not happy in our jobs, we can become trapped by our loyalty. We can be selfless to a fault. We often forget that we have the power to make things better for ourselves. We are not trapped in any particular job or any particular pond, but we are often trapped by our own insecurities and our inaccurate thinking.

We sometimes wrongly believe that the top management people in our organization know what is best for us, and that they will act accordingly. Like the fish in the story, we swim where they tell us to swim and we eat what they give us to eat. We rarely make a fuss over things for fear of stirring up the waters.

All too often, we forget to take charge of our own careers. We leave our future in the hands of other people rather than taking charge of it ourselves. We ignore the underground streams that could take us to other ponds, or we are too afraid or guilt-ridden to explore them. We forget that we have free will.

As I'm sure you suspect, many men do not share our fear or our guilt. They move to new ponds through the underwater streams, whenever it's in their best interest to do so. I'm not suggesting that we should emulate our male colleagues, but when it comes to self-preservation, we might want to take a lesson from them.

I fully recognize that not all women aspire to be a big fish, and not all women want to swim in a big pond. That's good because a pond's survival depends on the productivity of a lot of satisfied little fish. There is nothing wrong with being a happy little fish in a cozy little pond or a comfortable big pond. Being a big fish is not for everyone. One size does not fit all.

The challenge embedded in the parable is to examine your own career ambition and to reflect on your authentic self. What size fish do you really want to be? What size pond is ideal for you? The exercise on the following page is designed to help you figure this out.

This chapter's parable is designed to remind you how uncomplicated the most important lessons in life can be. Quite simply, Phoebe and Franny call you to be true to who you are. They call you to take action to become the kind of fish that you want to be and in the pond that's right for you. Your success and your sanity depend on it.

EXERCISE

The following exercise was designed to help you examine your individual work history as it relates to the big fish little pond effect.

Step 1

Make a list of all the professional jobs that you've held including your current job (if the list is longer than five, then list your five most recent jobs). For each job, list your job title and the name of the organization you worked for on the following worksheet.

Step 2

Choose which of the following categories best described your situation within that job:

Fish/Pond Categories:

a) Big Fish in a Big Pond

b) Big Fish in a Little Pond

c) Little Fish in a Big Pond

d) Little Fish in a Little Pond

Mark your answer under the heading "Fish/Pond Category" on the following worksheet.

Step 3

Rate your professional success and personal sanity at each of the jobs listed on the worksheet. Mark your answers under each heading "Success" and "Sanity."

Success and Sanity Rating Scale:

1= Very Good

2 = Good

3 = Poor

Job Title /Organization	Fish/Pond Category	Success & Sanity Rating
1.		/
2.		/
3.		/
4.		/
5.		/

Step 4

Examine your answers on the worksheet and consider the following questions?

- Do you have a consistent pattern of fish/pond categories or have you experienced a variety of different ones?

- Which categories have brought you the greatest success and sanity?

- What was it about those jobs that gave you the greatest success or sanity? Was it the size of the fish or the pond or some other combination of factors that made things work well for you?

- Which fish/pond categories have brought you the least success and sanity?

- What was it about that job that gave you the least success or sanity? Was it the size of the fish or the pond or some other combination of factors that made things work not as well for you?

- Is there one particular category that you think would be a good fit for you that you have not yet had an opportunity to try? What is it about this category that appeals to you?

Step 5

As you consider new job opportunities in the future, think about which fish/pond category the new job opportunity fits into. Have you experienced that category before and if so, how did it work out for you? Is it a new category that you've always wanted to try?

As part of your decision making process, recall the parable of Phoebe Fish and remember the importance of choosing the fish/pond category that brings out the best in you!

chapter

Six Degrees of Separation in Organizations

I'm sure that many of you have heard of the trivia game "Six Degrees of Kevin Bacon." The game is based on the concept that any actor can be linked through his or her film roles to Kevin Bacon in six or fewer steps.

The game was created in 1994 by three students at Albright College after Kevin Bacon commented in an interview that he'd worked with everyone in Hollywood or someone who'd worked with them.

In the Kevin Bacon version of the game, President Ronald Reagan is only two degrees away from Kevin Bacon.

- Ronald Reagan was in *The Young Doctors* (1961) with Eddie Albert.

- Eddie Albert was in *The Big Picture* (1989) with Kevin Bacon.

SIX DEGREES OF SEPARATION

The concept of six degrees of separation is actually based on the small world experiments conducted by famous sociologist Stanley Milgram in the 1960s. His groundbreaking research revealed that human society is a small world type network. The phrase, "six degrees of separation" is often associated with Milgram's experiments, although he never used the term himself.

The concept states simply that if a person is one step away from each person he or she knows and two steps away from each person who is known by one of the people he or she knows, then everyone is an average of six steps away from each person on Earth.

In the corporate version of the game, each employee is so many degrees of separation away from the Chief Executive Officer (CEO), who is by definition, the center of the corporate universe. I will use the term CEO here, but you should insert whatever title is appropriate for the top person in your organization. Also, if you are in a very large organization, you might want to think of the head of your division versus the overall CEO if your division functions fairly autonomously.

To calculate your degrees of separation, look at your company's organizational chart. How many steps does it take for you to reach the top person?

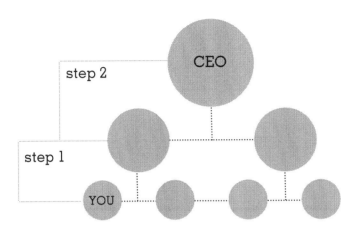

THE CENTER OF POWER AND INFLUENCE

Picture the top person in your organization as a bull's-eye on a target. That person is the center of power and influence. Each concentric circle moving away from the target is one degree of separation away from the center of power and influence.

The first ring of people, those with one degree of separation from the CEO, are among the most powerful and influential people in the organization. They are typically C-level executives like the Chief Operating Officer (COO), Chief Financial Officer (CFO), and various Vice Presidents or Senior Vice Presidents (depending on the structure of your organization.)

The Center of Power and Influence

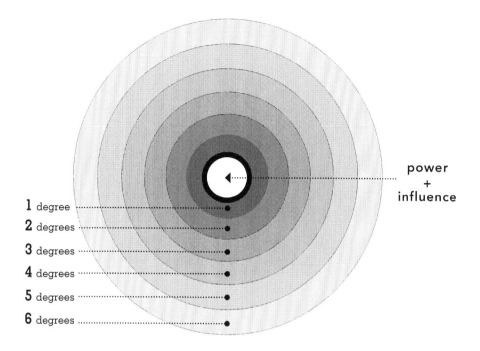

power
+
influence

1 degree
2 degrees
3 degrees
4 degrees
5 degrees
6 degrees

People with one degree of separation make major decisions for the organization. They have the CEO's ear. This does not mean they are the smartest or most hard working employees (although sometimes they are), it simply means that they participate in the strategic decisions that impact the organization.

The next ring of people have two degrees of separation away from the CEO. They typically still have some power and influence, though less than the people with one degree of separation.

In most organizations, these people are Vice Presidents or Executive Directors. They are generally not invited to the top-level meetings, but they are typically told about important decisions before they are rolled out to the rest of the organization.

As you would expect, power and influence decrease with each additional degree of separation away from the CEO.

By the time you get to four or five degrees of separation, you have little to no power or influence overcompany decisions. You are lucky if the CEO knowsyour name.

It does not mean you are not important to your organization. You might play a very important role. It simply means that you are not asked to participate in making important company decisions.

CALCULATING YOUR DEGREES OF SEPARATION

The following example is from my first professional job.

Me ➡ My boss ➡ Her boss ➡ His boss ➡ The President

By counting the arrows, you can see that I was four degrees of separation away from the President.

EXERCISE

1. Currently, how many degrees of separation are there between you and the top person ? ....

2. How many degrees of separation were there in your first job?..

3. How many degrees of separation were there in the job that brought you the most success? The most sanity? Both?...

During the first half of my corporate career I was promoted several times. I moved from four degrees of separation to two. I was headed in the right direction for me. I changed companies (moved to a smaller pond) to give myself a greater chance of getting ahead. It worked.

I made it to the top executive team. I was one degree of separation away from the CEO of the smaller pond. This was by far my most challenging, exciting, and fulfilling corporate position.

A big part of that was the amazing corporate culture at the time, but another big part was my power and influence within the organization. I enjoyed the responsibility and rewards of being part of a strategic leadership team. I liked being a player in the important meetings. I liked being a part of the team that ran the company.

During the last few years of my corporate career our little pond went through two mergers and acquisitions. I became part of a much bigger pond and I moved from one degree of separation from the CEO to three.

My new position was considered a promotion because I had gone from a Vice President in a $40 million dollar organization to a Vice President in a $300 million dollar organization.

It's true that I had a much greater span of responsibility; I had many more people reporting to me, and I was making more money. However, none of these factors made up for my decreased lack of power and influence.

It's somewhat ironic that the people who tell you that you should not care about your place on the organizational chart are always the people above you on the organizational chart. It's easy for them to say that position should not matter, but it does.

chapter

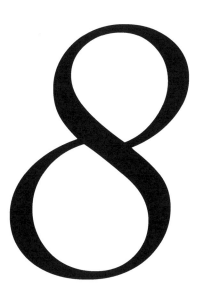

Corporate Culture:
What's the Right Fit for You?

When I am asked what one piece of advice I would pass along to professional women seeking a job it would be – consider corporate culture in your decision making process just as seriously as you consider job title, salary, bonuses, healthcare, vacation, and retirement benefits.

Culture is just another name for an organization's personality. An organization's culture is the underlying (and often unspoken) set of accepted rules and norms that bind members of an organization together.

Just like with human personalities, an organization's personality is deeply rooted and consistent over time. It has a strong influence on the way the organization's people think, interact, and behave.

Most of us would agree that we get along better with certain types of people because of the fit between our personality and theirs. We tend to gravitate toward people who bring out the best in us.

The same can be said of organizations. They have a personality type too, and we should gravitate toward the ones that bring out the best in us.

To borrow from a common idiom, a square peg does not fit into a round hole, but it fits nicely into a square one. Without changing anything about the shape of the peg, we can find a better fit for it simply by changing where we place the peg.

Similar logic applies to your success and sanity. You can increase your overall success and sanity without changing a single thing about yourself, by simply finding an organization with a culture that is right for you. That's what makes corporate culture so important. Obviously finding the right fit is not always easy, but the payoff is well worth the effort.

THE CORPORATE LENS

Imagine corporate culture like the lens on a camera. The lens is the filter through which everyone and everything in the company is viewed. An employee's professional skills, for example, are not inherently valuable, but are only valuable in so much as they are perceived as valuable through the company's lens. The same skills may be extremely valuable in one organization and only moderately valued in another. It's all about finding the right fit.

CHARACTERISTICS OF CORPORATE CULTURE

If you have worked for several different organizations, you can undoubtedly think of numerous characteristics that differentiated one culture from another. I have selected seven of the most highly distinguishable characteristics of corporate culture to highlight in this chapter.

Each characteristic is represented by two categories. While the two categories are presented as mutually exclusive options (Category A versus Category B) most organizations have some combination of both. That is why it's important to think of each characteristic along a continuum.

A NOTE ABOUT MY CATEGORY BIAS

Most of you are probably familiar with the Myers-Briggs Type Indicator (MBTI), arguably the most widely used personality inventory in the world today. The developers of the MBTI take great effort to assure people that all personality types are created equal. One type is not better than another, they are just different. Most personality tests adopt a similar judgement-free perspective. The characteristics I describe in this chapter do not. My bias toward the characteristics listed in Category A will become clear when you read the descriptions. The bias is based on my own personal experiences and preferences and does not imply what's right for other women.

When you read the descriptions below, think about which category feels right for you. Which description are you drawn to and why? Which one seems like the right match for your professional personality? Remember these are on a continuum not either/or choices.

After reading the next pages, you can record your preferences at the end of the chapter.

CHARACTERISTIC	CATEGORIES A vs. B
1. Communication	Inclusive vs. Exclusive
2. Leadership	Inspiring vs. Intimidating
3. Focus	Internal vs. External
4. Values	Mission vs. Money
5. Flexibility	Flexible vs. Inflexible
6. Rewards	Results vs. Time
7. Pace	Entrepreneurial vs. Traditional

1. COMMUNICATION

- How does the company communicate information to employees?

- What kinds of information do they share with employees?

- How do employees communicate with each other?

Category A) Inclusive Communication

Companies with an inclusive culture have an informal communication style. There are not a lot of formal meetings or corporate memos.

Top management is visible and approachable. There is an open door policy. Employees are encouraged to discuss their ideas with management. There is little emphasis on hierarchy, status, or title.

Information is readily shared among all employees (including information about the company's financial performance). Employees communicate with each other in an open and honest fashion without posturing or finger-pointing.

Category B) Exclusive Communication

Companies with an exclusive culture are more secretive and closed in their communication style. Knowledge is considered power and only those in top management are given access to the knowledge. Individual employees are informed about important company issues on a "need-to-know" basis.

Management shields employees from difficult issues or bad news. They feel it is their responsibility to run the business for the good of all employees. When difficult information is shared, it is done in a more formal fashion.

There is little direct communication or interaction between upper management and the average employee in companies with an exclusive culture. Upper management is less visible and less approachable. Meetings between management and non-management employees require an appointment with a specific purpose.

Employees often use their title or status as leverage when communicating with each other. Hierarchy is important.

2. LEADERSHIP STYLE

- What is the leadership style of the people in power?

- What strategies do leaders use to motivate employees?

Category A) Inspiring

Leaders in companies with an inspiring culture use encouragement as a way to motivate employees. They lead by example. They inspire employees to become the best they can be.

Inspiring leaders welcome the opportunity to coach and mentor high potential employees. They help employees stretch and grow by believing in them and recognizing their professional strengths. As you'll read in Chapter 13, inspirational leadership is the top quality women seek in their leaders.

Category B) Intimidating

Leaders in companies with an intimidating culture use fear as a way to motivate people. Fear of public humiliation or job loss is what drives employees to perform.

In the extreme, intimidating leaders keep a distance from employees. They delight in publicly humiliating people. They look for opportunities to finger-point and assign blame.

Note: I reluctantly use the word "leader" here as people who use fear and intimidation are not deserving of the title leader. This category is also the exception to the rule that every category is the right fit for someone. I have yet to meet a professional woman who benefits from a culture of fear and intimidation.

3. FOCUS

- Where do employees focus the majority of their time and talents?

Category A) Internally focused

Companies with an internally focused culture devote most of their attention to the internal operations of the company. They measure and report on a variety of internal metrics. They closely adhere to standardized company policies and procedures.

Internally focused companies tend to value the opinions of their own upper management much more than they listen to the opinions of their clients or the market. Employees rarely spend time outside the office interacting with customers.

Companies going through significant changes in upper management, major organizational restructuring, or a merger and acquisition often become internally focused (at least temporarily) even if they are not customarily internally focused.

Category B) Externally focused

Companies with an externally focused culture pay close attention to their clients. They are constantly re-evaluating their processes based on client feedback. Client satisfaction and retention is their top priority.

All employees are expected to really know their clients and their competition. The focus is outward.

4. VALUE

- What does the company value?

- What drives the employees?

- Where is their passion?

Category A) Mission-based

Companies with a culture that is based on a mission, value their core beliefs over their financial gains. The company feels like it has a purpose and a soul, when it has a mission driven culture.

Author Bo Burlingham profiles several mission-driven companies in his book, *Small Giants*. Burlingham gives examples of companies who choose to stay small and remain true to their mission, rather than capitalize on large financial returns, and risk losing their mission.

Employees who work for a mission-driven company often feel a special sense of pride in their work. They believe their work has purpose. They have a deep connection and loyalty to their company, beyond the paycheck.

Many women find mission driven companies a preferred place to work because the company's mission resonates with them and gives their work meaning.

Category B) Money-based

Companies with a culture based on money value financial performance over everything else. All decisions are made with a specific purpose of meeting financial goals. Revenue and the bottom line are the language spoken by leaders in a money-driven culture.

The decisions can appear arbitrary or short-sighted, when they are based on meeting financial goals rather than on serving a long-term mission.

5. WORK SCHEDULE FLEXIBILITY

- How flexible is the company when it comes to employee schedules?

Category A) Flexible

Companies with a flexible work culture recognize that employees have a life outside of work. They accommodate a variety of schedules to meet employees' needs.

A flexible work culture can include everything from part-time schedules and job sharing to working from home or working in other remote locations.

A flexible culture recognizes that giving the employee flexibility wins loyalty and increases employee performance enormously.

Category B) Inflexible

Companies with an inflexible culture do not allow employees to adjust their own work schedules. They have intolerance for flexible work arrangements and have strict policies in place to safeguard against them.

They view the desire for flexibility as a sign of weakness or lack of commitment on the employee's part. They do not believe that work should accommodate an employee's life.

Vacation time is often limited and carefully monitored in companies with inflexible cultures. Employees are expected to use their time-off for everything from attending a child's school function to attending a dentist appointment. The company applies their inflexible rules consistently to all employees to be fair.

6. REWARD SYSTEM

- What does the company recognize and reward among its employees?

Category A) Results-based

Companies with a results-oriented culture reward employees for what they do, not for how much time they spend doing it. They reward performance, deliverables, and tangible results.

A results-oriented culture has clear objectives upon which employees are evaluated. Bonuses and promotions are based on an employee's results, not on the amount of time she spends at the office.

Taken to the furthest extreme, a results-oriented company operates in a Results-Only-Work-Environment (ROWE) as described by Cali Ressler and Jody Thompson in their book, *Why Work Sucks and How to Fix It*. In this type of culture, employees can do whatever they want, whenever they want, as long as the work gets done.

Category B) Time-based

Companies with a time-oriented culture place a high value on the amount of time that employees spend in the office. They perceive time in the office as a direct indication of an employee's dedication and worth.

Top credit goes to the employee who spends the most time at the office, regardless of the results she produces. Employees compete to see who can arrive first at work, leave last, and spend the most time in the office on weekends.

This type of culture is counter-intuitive for younger generations. They are accustomed to sitting in a coffee shop with their laptops, focusing on getting things accomplished and not on punching the clock.

When I talk with younger professionals, they are often very surprised to learn that their company might actually care more about how much time they spend at the office than what they produce.

Time-oriented companies value employees who are known and recognized by the top leaders. This can be especially challenging for employees who work in a remote location away from the center of power and influence. These employees are at a significant disadvantage because it's difficult to build name recognition and get credit for the time you're in the office, when the important people don't see you at the office.

Time is a valuable commodity for all employees, but it is an especially valuable commodity for many working women. Many men appear to have a greater luxury of time on their side. They are in the office at the end of the day without any apparent urgency to go home. On the other hand, many women have family obligations that drive them out the door in a whirlwind at a specific time each day.

Fortunately, women have the ability to multi-task in a way men do not making them ideally suited for producing rapid results. However, the time-oriented culture is a disadvantage for women because it still values time over results.

Imagine the following scenario:

A professional woman and a professional man are each given the exact same project to complete. Their results are the same. The woman takes 8 hours to complete the task and the man takes 10 hours.

In a time-based culture, the man is perceived as the superior employee because he spent more time in the office. The woman is penalized for her efficiency.

Some clever employees even find ways to beat time-oriented companies at their own game. They occupy extra time at the office with personal projects like paying bills or playing computer games.

Unfortunately, I've seen more than one shrewd employee get credit for their long hours spent at work when credit was not due. For better or worse, time spent at the office is still what matters most in organizations that value time over results.

7. PACE OF DECISION-MAKING

- How quickly does everything from decisions to promotions happen within the company?

Category A) Entrepreneurial

Companies with an entrepreneurial culture operate at a fast pace. They are willing to make quick decisions in the spirit of innovation. They prefer to try new things and fail, rather than to not to try new things at all.

Promotional tracks are also more rapid for employees in these companies. High achieving employees can expect to climb the corporate ladder more quickly than they would in a more traditional company. There are not established rules, guidelines of protocols, determining the pace of promotions in an entrepreneurial company.

On the other hand, processes are often not well documented in an entrepreneurial culture and changes can happen very quickly and without much notification.

Employees need to stay alert to keep up with the changes. Decisions can feel like they are made in haste when they are made so quickly. The fast pace is not ideal for everyone.

Category B) Traditional

Companies with a traditional culture operate at a slower, more methodical pace. They think through decisions long and hard before making changes.

They are more risk-averse. Promotions, like everything else in the organization, follow standard protocols and are much slower to happen.

WHICH CHARACTERISTICS DO YOU PREFER?

Step 1: Place an X along the continuum below labeled **"You"** where you believe your professional personality best fits that particular characteristic. Your professional personality is your personality at work which may or may not be the same as your personality at home.

Step 2: Place an X along the continuum marked **"Org"** where you believe your current organization's personality fits for that particular characteristic.

Step 3: Repeat the process for each of the seven characteristics. A midline is provided along each continuum as a reference point. It represents an equal mix of both characteristics.

Example:

You: Inclusive ....X................ ▲ .... Exclusive

Org: Inclusive .... ▲ .... X .... Exclusive

---

1. Communication

You: Inclusive............................... ▲ ....Exclusive

Org: Inclusive............................. ▲ ....Exclusive

2. Leadership Style

You: *Inspiring...............................▲...........................Intimidating*

Org: *Inspiring...............................▲...........................Intimidating*

3. Focus

You: *Internal ....▲.................................External*

Org: *Internal ....▲.................................External*

4. Values

You: *Mission ....▲.................................. Money*

Org: *Mission ....▲.................................. Money*

5. Work Schedule Flexibility

You: *Flexible...............................▲..................................Inflexible*

Org: *Flexible...............................▲..................................Inflexible*

6. Reward System

You: *Results ....▲... Time*

Org: *Results ....▲... Time*

7. Pace of Decision-Making

You: *Entrepreneural ....▲............................... Traditional*

Org: *Entrepreneural ....▲............................... Traditional*

Fill in other characteristics that are meaningful to you:

8.   _____

9.   _____

10. _____

REVIEWING YOUR RESULTS

- How closely do your responses between you and your organization compare?

- Which characteristics have the closest match?

- Which characteristics are the farthest apart?

- Which characteristics are most important to you?

- Which characteristics do you believe are most important to your organization?

- Do the characteristics with greatest discrepancy create an annoyance for you at work or do they create more of a true roadblock to your overall achievement and job satisfaction?

- If they are a roadblock, what strategies can you put in place to overcome the roadblocks?

BOTTOM LINE

An organization's personality (referred to as its culture) is one variable beyond your control that has the most influence on your success, sanity, and overall satisfaction at work.

If an organization's culture is the right fit for you, then your talents will shine and the work environment will bring out the best in you.

If it's not a good fit, then your talents (brilliant as they might be) will be overlooked and undervalued.

A company's culture is not permanent, but it certainly is deeply rooted. The culture is not likely to change with the typical ebb and flow of employee attrition, but is more likely to change when there are major changes in top management.

Since a company's culture has such an enormous impact on the way your skills and abilities are perceived, it just makes good sense to take a serious look at it.

chapter

The Linear Career Track: Is It Your Only Option?

When I was 18 years old I worked at Kings Island Amusement Park. It was the one certain place that Cincinnati teenagers could get a summer job with no experience required. Everyday on my way to the park's pizzeria where I worked, I walked past a roller coaster called the Racer.

The Racer held the record for world's fastest roller coaster during the mid 1970s, and by the early 1980's people were still willing to stand in line a very long time to ride it. I rode it several times myself that summer. I vividly remember the excitement of finally getting to the front of the line, maneuvering into my seat, and waiting for the heavy metal seatbelt to lower into place – a signal that the thrill was about to begin.

Our careers are not all that different than a ride on the Racer. We wait in line a very long time to take our turn (Kindergarten through college, or graduate school for many of us). Once we are seated, the momentum of the coaster propels us into a continuous forward motion with no built in pauses or breaks. The ride is both exhilarating and unnerving. Ironically, the very seatbelt that gives us a sense of security at the beginning of the ride can lead to a feeling of constraint later on. We come to realize that once the seatbelt is locked in place, it's almost impossible to get off the ride.

At some point in your career you may want to or need to get off the ride. Can you? Is there a way to stop the forward momentum – for just a little while? Is there a way to stop the ride and get back on without having to wait in line again? In other words, is it ever possible for women to take a time-out from their careers without sacrificing their success?

OFF-RAMPS AND ON-RAMPS IN WOMEN'S CAREERS

In a groundbreaking study called "The Hidden Brain Drain: Off-Ramps and On-Ramps in Women's Careers" (published by *Harvard Business Review Research Report*, March 2005) Dr. Sylvia Ann Hewlett and her colleagues report the following key findings about time-outs:

- A substantial number of highly qualified women voluntarily leave their careers for a period of time (37%).

- Even short time-outs can be extremely costly for women. On average, women lose 18% of their earning power when they off-ramp for less than three years and that goes up to 37% when they off-ramp for three or more years.

- Coming back to work is very challenging for women once they leave. Fully 93% of women currently off-ramped want to get back to work, yet fewer than 74% are successful in obtaining jobs – and only 40% of these jobs were full-time.

While the literature suggests that it's very difficult for women to take any type of time-out and come back to the job they held before, the reality is that there may be a time in your career when you want, or need to take a time out. Maternity leave is usually considered an exception to the no time-out rule as long as the leave does not exceed the duration permitted by an organization's standard policies and practices.

The important message for women is to start preparing for a possible time-out now. Take advantage of the times when you have fewer personal demands in your life and channel your energy at work. Build up your goodwill so that if you need to take a time-out, you have a solid reputation and lots of built up goodwill.

Taking a break does not always mean completely walking away from work or giving up your responsibilities for a position that is less demanding. Sometimes it means just getting some relief from the stress of your current position by delegating tasks or bringing on additional support to help with your work load.

CASE STUDY: SOPHIE'S STORY

The title of this chapter begs the question: When, if ever, is it acceptable for a woman to take a time-out? Sophie asked me that exact same question soon after she was diagnosed with breast cancer. She had started a new job just months before her diagnosis, and her new employer was terrific about accommodating all her time-off for surgery, chemotherapy, and daily radiation.

Sophie worked from a satellite office and found that her remote location, combined with her illness, created a feeling of isolation that was unfamiliar and uncomfortable to her. When a new job with less responsibility opened up within her organization, she applied for it.

Sophie called me and asked whether I thought it was wrong for her to want the easier job. She questioned if she was backing down from a challenge in her current job and selling herself short in her career. In the new job, she would have no direct reports and less stress. Prior to her illness, she had been a director of a department and had immense responsibility. She was one of the high-performing, high-potential up-and-coming women leaders within her organization. She questioned why she was so willing to accept less responsibility now.

In talking to Sophie, I realized that her own guilt about seeing this as a step backward professionally stood in the way of her feeling good about accepting the job – even if accepting it was a step forward for her sanity.

If this new job was the "easy way out," was that such a bad thing under the circumstances? Isn't it reasonable to assume that a woman who is dealing with cancer might need to trade in a little success for greater sanity?

Sophie is the perfect example of an employee that needs a break from her highly demanding job. Not forever, just temporarily. Her time-out did not entail actual time away from the office, bur rather, time away from the demands of her current position. Sophie's desire to step back from her current situation was completely reasonable and her company did a good job in facilitating that.

If more companies were better at helping women through tough transition times in their lives, then they would be more likely to gain loyalty from the very women leaders that they are trying to retain.

The true test for Sophie's company, and others like hers, is how they handle things after the crisis passes. Women like Sophie need a temporary time-out, but they usually do not want the time-out to last forever. Managers that fail to give women like Sophie the chance to get back on their previous career tracks when they are ready are missing out on proven and much needed talent.

NAVIGATING YOUR TIME-OUT

Before you ask your employer for a temporary time-out, consider exactly what you want your time out to look like.

- Are you hoping to take a short time-out before returning to your current job position?

- Are you hoping to take a short time-out before returning to a job position with less responsibility than the position you hold today?

- Are you hoping to take a longer time-out before returning to work in an undetermined position?

Once you know what you're hoping to accomplish, take a look around your organization and see if there are any people who have successfully done what you are hoping to do. If there are, how did they do it? What can you learn from their experiences? Are there Human Resource (HR) policies in place that will either support or derail your plans?

If there are policies in place to help facilitate the type of career time-out you are looking for, but no one has ever actually acted upon the policies, then accept your position as a pioneer (or guinea pig) and be willing to accept the challenges and uncertainty that come with that role.

If you are in a position to manage people, be sure to recognize that there are times when your top employees may need to take a time-out for a day, a week, a month, or longer. Do you have strategies in place to allow this to happen? If not, start putting a plan in place today.

You would rather be in a position to accommodate a top employee's request to take a time-out than to lose her all together if her only choice is to stay on her current career path or drop out completely.

THE LINEAR CAREER TRACK

Corporate America will tell you that career tracks are linear, and my experience confirms that most of the time they are. Each position you hold is designed to lead you to the next one, and the one after that. You generally don't move backwards, once you've moved ahead.

Your company expects you to have ambition. They expect you to jump at the next available promotion. I always did, so it never occurred to me that someone else would not. Then I met Kirk. I offered Kirk a desirable promotion within my department and without hesitation he turned it down.

What reasons did he give? He very matter-of-factly stated that he did not want to work that hard. He perceived the new job as more work than he cared to take on. What exactly did that mean? The new job did not involve relocation, it did not involve additional travel, it did not involve a significantly longer work week. So what exactly about the new job caused Kirk to think it would be too much work?

Kirk accurately realized that the new job would require him to take his performance to the next level. It would put him under the microscope in a way that he had not been before. For those reasons he saw it as too much work, and turned it down.

Kirk had been invited to become a leader in the organization and he declined. My boss was stunned when I told him the news. He had thought very highly of Kirk, but I can guarantee you his opinion of him changed immediately. By declining the promotion, Kirk had taken himself off the list of rising stars. His chances for further professional advancement within the company ended the minute he declined the promotion.

Why is declining a promotion not well accepted in corporate America?

- Corporate America wants their employees to be eager and hungry.

- Corporate America frowns on complacency.

- Corporate America is not ready for their leaders to choose sanity over success.

EXTRA PAY FOR EXTRA WORK? NOT NECESSARILY

Good news. You're offered a promotion at work. You're excited about the new responsibilities and the increase in pay. Hold on. Don't assume that the promotion means more money. It may or it may not.

Some companies pay by salary bands and if your new job moves you into a higher salary band, you may expect to see a raise attached to it. Other companies have a "pay for performance" philosophy which means that they do not pay you upfront for taking on more responsibility. They wait to see how well you perform and then pay for exceptional performance.

It's very true that as women we are not good about asking for more money for ourselves even when we should. But before you ask for more money every time you're given additional responsibilities, ask yourself the following question:

"Does this change in responsibilities really warrant an increase in my salary?" Here are some guidelines to help you evaluate your answer:

- If your title is changing in a significant way (i.e., going from a director to an executive director for example, or director to Vice President) then you can rightfully expect a raise.

- If the number of direct reports you have changes dramatically (i.e., going from none to some or from some to a lot), then it's completely reasonable to ask for a raise.

- If you are being asked to relocate or to increase your travel extensively, then it's appropriate to ask for a pay raise.

- However, if you're taking on additional responsibilities that do not dramatically change your daily routine, then you should not expect an increase in pay. You don't want to be labeled as the employee who asks for more money every time she is offered additional responsibilities.

In general, I do not recommend that women take on significantly more job responsibilities without increased pay because I don't believe men do it. However, in light of the story of Kirk (who was forever marginalized after declining the promotion) you have to weigh the risk of turning down new opportunities that are presented to you, even if these opportunities come with marginal or no pay increase. Taking the promotion may not be the right choice for you, and that's fine, as long as you realize that

Hint: When you take on additional responsibility, consider asking for another week of vacation time, flex time, or a one-time bonus, rather than a salary increase. My friends in human resources taught me that companies are often much more willing to negotiate on these terms than they are on base salary.

your choice will most likely have negative consequences within your current organization.

DELAYED GRATIFICATION

Sometimes the payoff for taking on additional work is not immediate. That happened to me when I became a Vice President. I had taken on numerous additional responsibilities as a director without an increase in pay, but without those experiences I would not have been in a position to get the Vice President's job. Therefore, taking on additional responsibility without pay eventually had a big reward. Sometimes you have to be patient and accept delayed gratification.

However as a word of caution, waiting is not the same thing as asking for nothing. If you ask for nothing, you'll get nothing. You need to ask, even if you're told you have to wait. Don't shy away from these sometimes difficult conversations. I can guarantee you the men in your office are not shying away from them. Be a strong advocate for your own financial worth and ask for what is fair and equitable.

IT'S ABOUT CONTROL

Looking back on the situation with Kirk, I sometimes wonder why the company did not think it was acceptable for him to turn down the promotion. Was it because he was male? I don't think so. I don't think upper management would have been any more tolerant of a high-potential woman declining the promotion. I think it's a matter of control.

Companies want to be in control of who works at what level. They want to decide who is worthy of promotion and they want employees to go along with their decisions. When an employee declines a promotion, they are challenging the company's control, and that makes the management of the company uncomfortable.

If you are identified as a rising star, then you are expected to want the promotions that go along with that label. If you are not identified, then the company wants you to remain happy at the level they assign to you. Companies need future leaders, but they also need productive, happy followers. It really comes down to a company's ability to control the human capital in their pipeline.

DO YOU KNOW WHAT EXPECTATIONS YOUR ORGANIZATION HAS OF YOU?

This brings up an interesting question. Do you have any idea what level your company has in mind for you? Have you ever been told or have you ever asked what career path the company sees for you? Everyone talks about how you need to manage your own career, and you do. But the truth is, your career is a two-way conversation and you can't manage it without information about what your company thinks of you. If you don't fit their mold, or their profile, you won't advance no matter how hard you try.

- Have you made your boss aware of what expectations you have for yourself?

- Do your expectations of yourself match your companies expectations of you?

I would urge you not to give your organization total control over what position you aspire to in your career. You should decide what position you aspire to and make sure you communicate that to your boss. Talk to her about the pathway you envision for yourself and make sure it's a pathway that she's willing to support you in as well.

All too often professional women believe that being a polite, dedicated, hard-working employee is enough to be rewarded. The truth is, if women ruled the world, these qualities might be rewarded more often. However, in today's competitive corporate environment, they are not. The squeaky wheel really does get the grease. Employees who draw attention to themselves (either for their accomplishments or their grievances) get rewarded far more often than employees who do not. How can your boss know you want more out of your job (more responsibility, more recognition, or more rewards) if you don't make those intentions known? A quiet employee is assumed to be a content employee. So, if you're not content—if you want more, you need to let your boss know that.

chapter

10

A Great Job

x   A Bad Organization

=   A BAD JOB

No job exists in a vacuum. A job is part of an overall organization and your feelings toward the organization will eventually have an impact on the way you feel about your job.

A great job in a bad company always equals a bad job. This equation is as simple as the basic math we learned in elementary school – a positive number times a negative number is always a negative number.

Why? It's pretty simple. If it's the right job for you, and it's a great job that you enjoy, chances are you will excel at it. As you excel, you will likely get promoted and receive additional responsibilities that draw you closer to the core of the company.

As you get closer to that core, you will be asked and expected to adopt, support, and promote the core values of the company. If you aren't in agreement with these, then your great job will start to deteriorate into a not-so-great job. Your happiness will be short-lived.

What makes a company a good or bad company? Inherently nothing. It's simply a matter of fit. Do you agree with the goals of the company? Do you take pride in the company? Do you admire the leaders? Do you believe in the overall strategic vision? Can you comply with the policies and procedures? If so, it's most likely a good company for you.

If it's the wrong company for you, then trying to make it the right company is practically impossible. It's like trying to take a sip of water out of a gushing fire hose. The task is overwhelming. I can guarantee you that you will not be able to compartmentalize the things that are great about your job forever if you dislike the company. Eventually, the influence of the company will creep in.

THE REALITY OF MANAGEMENT

People who are in management positions are expected to be on-board with the company's vision. That's a fact. Part of what you're being paid for in management is to be a good corporate citizen. This does not mean that you should not question things or voice your opinion. Part of what the company also pays you for is your perspective and your expertise.

At the end of the day, if you can't get on-board with the direction your company is headed, it's time to find a new ship. If in good conscience you can not implement the decisions that your organization makes, then you should not be part of the organization any longer. It's that simple.

This might be a bitter pill to swallow. You might think that it's okay to work behind the scenes ignoring company directives. You might even convince yourself that it's acceptable to collude with co-workers in the process. It is not. It's never okay to intentionally undermine the success of your organization.

While a particular company might not be the right company for you, it's the right company for many other people. No matter how disenchanted or angry you might be, you do not have the right to cause harm to other people's jobs.

HOW DID THINGS GO FROM GOOD TO BAD?

Most companies do not start out as a bad place for you to work. Most start out as a good place and then something happens to change them. What typically happens? How does the right company for you become the wrong company for you?

In my experience, these changes usually happen as a result of a major company reorganization, merger, acquisition, or changes in the senior management team. When the President, CEO, or senior management changes, you can be certain that other changes will follow. The higher up you are in an organization, the more quickly the changes typically roll down to you. Sometimes the changes are positive; sometimes they are negative. When they are negative your once-great company starts looking not so great anymore.

It can take several months or longer before unfavorable company changes have any impact on your opinion of the organization. Other times, your opinion can change overnight. Such is often the case when you're assigned a new boss - whom you deeply dislike. Having a boss that you don't respect is one of the primary reason professional women become dissatisfied with their organizations.

MOVING ON

Life's too short to be a high-achieving woman working for a company that isn't right for you. If you currently have a great job with a bad company, it's time to start thinking about finding a great job in a better company. Take time to think about what you like best about your current job and research other companies that may have similar positions.

If you can't find a great job in a good company, consider finding a good job in a good company instead. A good job in a good company may do more for your overall success and sanity than a great job in a bad company. Consider the pros and cons of the tradeoff.

I can tell you that throughout my many years in business, I have yet to meet a successful woman who stayed in a great job in the wrong company for very long. It just doesn't happen. It might take time for these women to find other jobs and leave, but eventually they do leave. If you're in a bad company, you should leave too.

THE EXCEPTION TO THE RULE

It would not be fair to end this chapter without considering the exception to the rule. Is it possible to have the right job in the wrong company? Perhaps, under the following circumstances:

You are a individual contributor – not in management; you never aspire to be in management. For instance, you might be a senior editor whose job is controlled in part by some standards separate from the individual organization (i.e., you comply with the standards of the written English language.) It seems possible for someone in this type of position to partially compartmentalize the great parts of her job from the bad parts of the company. However, even then, I would imagine that the organization plays a part in what kind of projects you're given and when those projects are due, so you are not working in a vacuum.

Or, maybe you work from your home or in a remote location with very little contact with the parts of your organization that make it the wrong place for you to work. Maybe you work for a really great department or division that is fairly autonomous from the overall organization. In this case, you might be able to sustain a great job in a bad company.

However, I offer a word of caution. I worked with a highly-skilled woman who was a director in one of our remote locations. She told me that she loved her job, but hated the company. She was removed from some of the day-to-day politics that drove her crazy, and that allowed her to stay longer than she might have, had she been located in the home office.

Eventually though, the politics that she hated took a toll on her sanity and she quit. She, like most women in her situation, found that a great job in a bad company eventually turns into a bad job.

chapter 10

chapter

11

Creating Your
Authentic Career

Think back to when you were in high school and college. What classes did you like the best? It was probably the ones in which you did very well. It's only natural that we like the things we are good at.

The same is true when it comes to our careers. We are drawn to the professions where we can excel. Our skills and abilities play a significant role in shaping our career choices. We gravitate toward the things we do best. Before we know it, we're into our career, sometimes without having given much thought to our full array of options.

At some point, we might start to feel like our true interests lie in a profession different than the one we're currently in. We face the reality that we would choose a different professional path if we could do it all over again. We feel trapped in an inauthentic career.

Have you ever felt this way? Olivia did. She is the perfect example of a successful woman trapped in an inauthentic career. Olivia's story highlights why it's important to factor your interests – not just your skills – into your overall success and sanity equation.

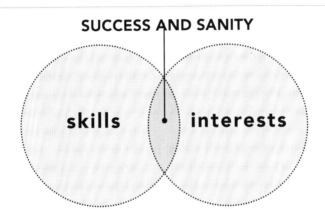

CASE STUDY: OLIVIA'S STORY

Olivia is a 30-year-old highly successful accountant. She has incredible talent and her career has been on the fast track for several years. If things continue as they have, she should expect to be offered a Chief Financial Officer (CFO) position in the near future. Great, right? Wrong. The problem? Olivia hates being an accountant. She wants to be a lawyer. Her passion is for the law and she get no enjoyment from her success as an accountant. She feels trapped by her success.

When Olivia is assigned work on a project with the lawyers in her company, she gets completely energized. She feels a connection with the lawyers that she does not feel with the accountants with whom she works. She's been told by lawyers that she thinks like a lawyer. She finds that many of the books she chooses to read for enjoyment are about the law.

LESSONS LEARNED

Olivia's story illustrates a very important point - skills alone do not create success and sanity in your life. If they did, Olivia would be a highly successful and very sane accountant, but she's not.

By traditional America standards, Olivia is quite successful. She has a prestigious and high paying job. Olivia does not disagree that she's doing very well financially. Money is not Olivia's problem. Authenticity is.

Olivia took the Leadhership1™ Success and Sanity Quiz (See Chapter 2). She rates her overall success and sanity as only a 2 on the 0 to 10 scale. What Olivia is missing in her life is a heartfelt connection with her career. She's missing the fun factor.

She has no enthusiasm for and no genuine enjoyment of her work. As a result, she finds the work draining no matter how naturally it comes to her. Olivia is on the promotional fast track because of her skills, but her work achievements are doing very little to contribute to her overall enjoyment of life.

CHANGE IS NOT WITHOUT EFFORT

Can you relate to Olivia? Do you feel inauthentic in your current career? If so, have you thought about making a change? The idea of making a major career change can be both exhilarating and frightening. Sometimes, it's difficult to admit to yourself and to the important people in your life that you want to try something different. The prospect can be especially tough if you've made a major investment of time, money and energy in your current career.

Tough as it can be to make a major career change, I am here to tell you that I've survived them twice, and you can too. I left medical school to pursue a PhD (major career change #1), and 17 years later I left a lucrative and fulfilling career as a corporate Vice President to start my own company (major career change #2).

These changes did not happen without significant soul-searching and tremendous effort. I faced the critics who thought, both times, that I had lost my mind. I can appreciate their perspectives, but I also know that each change led me to a more authentic place in my life. In my experience, authenticity is the only real foundation for building true success and sanity.

There is no shame discovering and re-discovering your interests throughout your life. There is strength in discovering that you want to try something new. The only shame is in perpetuating an inauthentic life. You will never discover the ultimate rewards of success and sanity in your life if you are trapped in an inauthentic career.

QUIZ

Take the following quiz to find out how authentic you feel in your current career.

Directions: Answer yes or no to each of the following questions. Circle your answer on the chart on page 174.

> **Note:** As you take the quiz, it's important to make a distinction between your *job* and your *career*. Your job is specific, while your career is general. In other words, your job takes into account your current organization, your boss and your colleagues, but your career only includes your overall profession. You can dislike your current job, but still enjoy your career. This quiz is about your career.

1. Is your current career the best one you can imagine for yourself?
    Yes   No

2. Do you spend time thinking about what career you'd choose if you could do it all over again?
    Yes   No

3. Are the talents that you enjoy using the ones that you use routinely in your current career?

   Yes　**No**

4. Do you feel like an outsider in your own career? In other words, does your interaction with the people in your profession feel unnatural or forced to you?

   Yes　**No**

5. Do you feel passionate about your work? Does your current career energize you on most days?

   Yes　**No**

6. Do you feel like there is a career out there that you're meant to be doing that you are not doing now?

   Yes　**No**

Scoring: Circle the Yes/No answer you selected above for each question to the corresponding Yes or No in the column below.

	Authentic	**Inauthentic**
Question 1	Yes	No
Question 2	No	Yes
Question 3	Yes	No
Question 4	No	Yes
Question 5	Yes	No
Question 6	No	Yes

A. Total up the number of answers circled in the **Authentic** column. **Total** = _____

B. Total up the number of answers circled in the **Inauthentic** column. **Total** = _____

Is one total greater than another or are they equal? Does your career look more authentic or inauthentic? If your career looks more inauthentic, what is keeping you from making it authentic?

Common roadblocks to finding a more authentic career include:

- You don't know what career might be better suited for you.

- You lack the confidence to pursue the career of your dreams.

- You feel financially trapped by your current salary.

- You lack the energy you need to make a change.

- You think that you are too old to start over again.

- You feel a sense of loyalty to your current career.

- You are uncomfortable admitting to others that you want to make a change. You fear they will be critical of your decision.

Whatever the reason, the bottom line is this: No highly-motivated, talented professional woman has to be trapped in an inauthentic career forever. You might not be able to switch gears tomorrow, but you can begin laying the foundation for the transition today.

TRANSITIONING FROM ONE CAREER TO ANOTHER

Changing jobs is much easier than changing careers. Changing careers can take time. The best way to approach a significant career change is to take the skills and abilities that you have in your current career and figure out how to best utilize those in your new career. Think of the transition as a bridge built with your passion and your most transferable skills.

In our example with Olivia, she can think about how to take her skills as an accountant and apply them to the field of law. She can capitalize on the fact that legal continuing education programs offer specific classes called "Accounting for Lawyers." Clearly it's an important topic for lawyers to understand in their practices.

With that said, once Olivia graduated from law school, she could market herself as a lawyer with an expertise in accounting. She might even decide to become in-house legal counsel for an accounting firm blending her knowledge of accounting with her passion for the law.

She may not have to quit her high-paying accounting job to go to law school if she can attend an evening or weekend law school program. Her successful transition to a new career will come from integrating her accounting skills with her authentic interest in the law.

HOW TO KNOW IF A CAREER IS RIGHT FOR YOU

Is there only one ideal career for you? Probably not. There are undoubtedly many different career options that would bring you success and sanity. Your goal is to find *a* right one, not *the* right one.

Lucky for us, career choices don't have to be forever. We did not make a commitment to stay with our career for-better-or-worse or until-death-us do-part. So, if you've outgrown your enthusiasm for your current career, it might be time to consider making a change.

Below are my top five pieces of advice for professional women who are considering a major career change.

1. Do your homework first. If possible, find a way to test the waters of a new career before you jump in. For example, find a way to participate in some sort of short-term internship (paid or unpaid) before you make the change. At the very least, interview people who are in your desired career and ask them for a realistic picture of what the career is all about. You don't want to be surprised.

2. Take your time. Major decisions should not be made in haste or from a place of confusion, anger, or irritation.

3. Engage the people who care about you the most in the decision- making process. Ask the advice of friends,

family members, mentors, and anyone you trust to have your best interest in mind. You should not be looking for consensus, but be open to their opinions.

4. Listen to your heart. Women have great intuition. Use it.

5. Keep you interests front and center in your decision making process. Remember that your skills will not be enough to bring you success and sanity in your new career. You need to have a sincere interest, if not a passion for the work you do, if you want success and sanity to follow.

Not all women are in a position to make major career changes regardless of how passionately they feel about a different career. That's absolutely true. Financial considerations are among the many factors that women need to take into account before making a change.

I encourage women to take all the time they need to explore their decision before making a significant career change. Be honest with yourself about both the pros and the cons of making a major change. Talk with people whose opinions you value.

Regardless of whether or not you are in a position to make a major career change in your life, I encourage all women who are feeling inauthentic in their careers to consider whatever changes they can make. Is there a project at work that is consistent with your interests? If so, ask to be assigned to it. Is there a group of people in your community who share your same career interests? If so, get to know them. Small changes are better than no changes at all when it comes to creating a more authentic life for yourself.

chapter

Attitude is Everything During Times of Change

The inscription on the sterling silver cigarette lighter reads "E.H. Davis – The Greatest. We'll miss you. From Hugh, Jackie, and Bob - June 1967." The lighter sits in my office today. It was a gift to my Grandfather upon his retirement from Laidlaw Books. The lighter reminds me how significantly times have changed in the working world, not simply because of the irony of an engraved cigarette lighter as a corporate thank you gift, but because my grandfather worked for the same company for 25 years.

Recent statistics suggest that people ages 18 to 38 will change jobs on an average of 10 times during their careers (Department of Labor). This statistic accounts for the number of times people change employers and/or the number of times people change jobs while working for the same employer.

The statistic does not take into account the number of times that changes are imposed on employees by an organization – change in management, change in strategic direction, change of ownership, etc. Add these types of changes to your list of voluntary job changes and the message becomes loud and clear – change is the name of the game for today's professionals. Your ability to respond effectively to change is essential to your sanity and your success.

NO ORGANIZATION IS EXEMPT FROM CHANGE

Organizations are constantly in a state of change. Whether your organization is big or small, public or private - change is inevitable. It is one of the trickiest and most repetitive themes you'll face in your career, so it's worth learning how to do right.

What does it take to be successful during time of change? In one word – attitude!

It may surprise you to learn that it's not your talent that matters most, but your willingness to embrace the changes as they happen.

I have experienced many corporate changes in my career, and I can guarantee you that attitude is the#1 thing that gets noticed by people in management. Attitude is everything.

There are two major types of changes – voluntary change and involuntary change.

- Voluntary changes are changes of your own choosing – like taking on more responsibility at work or accepting a new job.

- Involuntary changes are changes that you do not choose– like being laid off, going through a department restructuring, getting a new boss, or experiencing a merger and acquisition.

By definition, voluntary changes should be positive because you chose them. However, just because they are positive does not mean they are stress-free. Even positive changes cause stress.

Similarly, not all involuntary changes are negative simply because you did not choose them. Sometimes involuntary changes can result in significant growth opportunities that can be very positive for you.

WHAT'S THE BIG DEAL ABOUT ATTITUDE?

When you are making a voluntary change, you want to do it in a classy way. Let your attitude speak for itself. If you are choosing to leave your organization, your attitude is the lasting impression that your employer and your colleagues will have of you. Make it a good one.

During times of involuntary change attitude is equally, if not more, important. Change brings out the best and the worst in people. As long as the involuntary changes did not leave you unemployed, you want to be seen as open, agreeable, and responsive to the changes. If you are, you will be perceived as a more valuable employee. Your reaction to the changes will be remembered by your boss when it comes time for performance reviews, salary increases, or promotional opportunities.

Changes take a tremendous amount of time and energy on the part of the people charged with implementing the changes (typically upper management). Quite simply, they want the implementation to run as smoothly and successfully as possible. So they are looking for the people in the organization who will support their efforts. They are looking for the good corporate soldiers. They have no time, interest, or energy to spend converting the naysayers. Even the best and brightest employee who questions the changes can quickly be labeled as "disagreeable."

As a manager faced with mandatory staff reductions during times of change, I looked to attitude as an important factor in my decision making process. The people I suspected would be oppositional to the changes (based on their opposition to previous changes) were at the top of my reduction list.

I can't tell you whether or not you can, or should, in good conscience embrace all the changes that you will face during your career. I can tell you that when you do embrace changes, you will be noticed favorably. I've seen people with marginal talent get rewarded and recognized simply because they embraced difficult changes. Aptitude is important, but the truth is your willingness to be open and receptive to corporate changes will propel you further in many organizations than any other talents you bring to the table.

FOR MORE INFORMATION VISIT MY WEBSITE

If you are going through voluntary or involuntary job changes visit my website (www.leadhership1.com) for detailed information about how to navigate those changes successfully. The website contains specific advice, exercises and quizzes to help you:

- Understand your motivation for wanting to leave your current job.

- See how your personality, your qualifications, your references and luck impact your ability to land a job offer.

- Learn what not to do in an interview.

- Learn how to properly notify your current employer that you're quitting.

- Learn how to survive and thrive during a merger and acquisition.

- Understand what happens behind the scenes before most major corporate changes are announced.

chapter

13

Inspirational Leadership

Leadership is not about your place on the organizational chart. It's about the way you approach your work. Leadership can and should happen at every level in an organization.

Whether you have official responsibilities for managing people or not, you are capable of providing leadership to people within your organization. So don't just look to your boss for leadership, look to yourself.

WHAT DOES LEADERSHIP LOOK LIKE?

- Leadership is as much a state of mind as it is a list of prescribed behaviors.

- Leadership is as much about the character you display while accomplishing your work as it is about the actual work you accomplish.

In his bestselling 2003 book *Authentic Leadership*, Bill George (Former Chairman and CEO of Medtronic) introduces the concept of authentic leadership in response to the corruption of leaders at organizations like Enron and Arthur Andersen.

George advocates for a new generation of genuine and ethical business leaders. He calls for leaders to be committed to stewardship of their organization's assets and to making a difference in the lives of the people that they serve.

George's message resonates with me because serving others is something women do very well. Service to others is an innately female quality. George also advocates for leading with your heart as well as your head which is again consistent with a female perspective.

The notion of authentic leadership empowers working women to be true to who they are, without believing they need to become someone they are not. It calls women to be true to their core values. Authentic leadership is one of many characteristics that great leaders have in common.

I've compiled a list of another 20 characteristics, that in my experience, distinguish the great leaders from the average leaders. Some of the characteristics are applicable only to leaders who manage people, but others are applicable to leaders at every level of an organization.

Remember, leadership is not about having power. It's about having a positive influence on the lives of others, and we all have the potential for that every time we interact with our co-workers.

INSPIRATION AND INTEGRITY ARE TOP PRIORITY

More than any other single characteristic, working women are looking for leaders who inspire them. They want a leader who will help them to reach, grow, and achieve beyond what they imagined for themselves. They want a leader who motivates them to discover their own greatness.

Second on the working woman's list of priorities are leaders who have integrity. Leaders with integrity are trusted, respected, and admired. They lead by example and serve as role models and mentors for other working women.

As you read the list below, look for common themes. The themes provide important insight into the characteristics that women value most in their leaders, in themselves, and in their organizations.

After the top two spots, the list appears in no particular order of preference or importance.

A GREAT LEADER

- inspires others.

- has integrity.

- expects top performance in others because she demands it of herself.

- makes a personal connection with the people that she leads.

- is passionate about developing the future leaders of the organization. She has a gift for spotting raw talent and considers it a privilege to cultivate and support that talent.

- is a relentless advocate for her high performing employees.

- fights for issues that are important to her (and knows when it's time to keep her mouth shut, too).

- is an active listener. She has a genuine interest in what people are saying.

- helps create and nurture great teams.

- takes responsibility when things go wrong, but shares the credit when things go right.

- makes tough, and sometimes unpopular, decisions.

- earns the respect of people at all levels within her organization.

- has a vision that she communicates to others.

- seeks honest, constructive, and frequent feedback about herself.

- gives honest, constructive, and frequent feedback to her direct reports.

- leads by doing. She knows that her actions speak louder than her words.

- is a constant champion for her organization. And when she can no longer do that, a great leader knows it's time to move on.

- is the eye of the storm. She's the calm and dependable voice of reason, when chaos strikes.

- does not stifle employees' energy or enthusiasm by micromanaging them.

- re-energizes her mind and body with time away from work. She can not inspire people when she is mentally or physically exhausted.

EXERCISE

Look back over the list of 20 leadership qualities.

1. Put an "**O**" in the margin next to the ten qualities that you value the most in **Others.**

2. Next, put a "**Y**" in the margin next to the ten strongest leadership qualities that you see in **Yourself.**

3. Compare the qualities that you value most in others with the strongest qualities that you possess. Are there similarities?

4. If not, what can you do to develop the leadership qualities in yourself that you value most in others?

5. Do your leadership qualities come naturally to you or do they take effort on your part?

Working women often under-estimate the value of the characteristics that come most naturally to them. They wrongly assume if something comes naturally to them that it must come naturally to everyone. It may not. It's important to celebrate and utilize your natural gifts.

It's also important to stretch beyond your natural abilities and work hard to develop leadership skills that are outside of your comfort zone.

A great leader accepts the challenge to develop the characteristics that she admires the most in others, even when the characteristic seems well beyond her own natural abilities. With enough determination, these characteristics can become second nature to her, too.

- If you've never been a leader, I challenge you to become one.

- If you are already a leader, I challenge you to become a great leader.

- If you are already a great leader, I challenge you to become the kind of great leader who enthusiastically mentors the next generation of great leaders. They need you.

Madeleine Albright, the first woman to become the U.S. Secretary of State (under President Bill Clinton) is quoted as saying, "There is a special place in hell for women who do not help other women."

chapter

Lessons Learned From My Biggest Mistakes

To err is human. Believe me I know. I've been "human" at work more times than I care to remember. In this chapter, I recount four of my biggest professional blunders with the hope that you can learn from my mistakes.

MISTAKE #1 – WANTING PEOPLE TO LIKE ME

This mistake is very common among women because we are by nature people-pleasers. The truth is, there is nothing wrong with wanting people to like you. The mistake is in making decisions based on wanting people to like you.

Case-in-point: I was Vice President of a department that was responsible for protecting our company's intellectual property. As such, we had well-established guidelines and procedures that we followed. Many of the company's sales people disliked these procedures because they viewed them as unnecessary and cumbersome. It's true that the procedures did slow down a product's speed to market, but the trade off was invaluable legal protection for our company. So, we were strict about our adherence to the guidelines.

One day a veteran sales manager, Jessica, called me with a request for some changes that her client wanted on her program. I reminded Jessica that all changes needed to be submitted in writing, (with a client signature) before my department would act on the request.

Clearly annoyed, she reminded me of the long-standing working relationship that she had with this client. She assured me in a condescending tone that she would obtain his written confirmation the very next time she met with him.

Reluctantly, I agreed to make the changes before we received the client's signature. Why? Mostly because I was trying to get Jessica to like me. I was hoping that my gesture of goodwill would ease the antagonistic working relationship between our two departments. I convinced myself that it was okay to bypass the process this one time because Jessica had worked with this client for many years and I believed that she would eventually obtain his signature.

The problem is that she never did, and my good intentions backfired. Our long-standing client contact mysteriously resigned and was replaced by a man who demanded to know why we'd made the changes that we did. When we told him that the changes had been made at the direction of his predecessor, he told us to prove it - which we could not.

We did not have the documentation needed to justify our actions. We did not have the required client signature because I had not insisted on it. I had caved under the pressure of wanting to be liked. Eventually, the client took his business elsewhere and I felt like the blame rested squarely on my shoulders.

Lesson Learned: Leadership is not a popularity contest. Leaders make decisions that they know are right, regardless of how unpopular the decisions might be.

As unpopular as many of my subsequent decisions might have been, I never made that same mistake again. I stuck to the decisions that I believed were right. I do still care if people like me, but I no longer let that override my professional judgment.

MISTAKE #2 – TRYING TO FILL OTHERS' SHOES

Most of the time in business, your current job position was held by someone else prior to you. It's rare that your position is brand new. As such, there are empty shoes to fill when you start a new job and your natural assumption may be to try to fill the shoes the same way they were filled before (especially if your predecessor was well liked).

Case-in-point: Dennis was a very popular manager and had a very loyal following among his staff. From what I knew of his department, it ran like a well-oiled machine. I had no interest and no intention of taking Dennis's job. That is, until the day Dennis stormed out of work leaving behind his office keys and an open job position.

After much resistance on my part, my boss convinced me that taking the job was the right career move for me. I knew it would be tough to fill Dennis's shoes, but I set out to fill them nonetheless. First, I was convinced that I had to win the approval of his staff and secondly, I believed that I had to run the department just like he had run it.

There were several problems with my plan; not the least of which was trying to win the approval of a group of people who highly resented me for taking their boss's job (even though he had quit). They even presented a petition to our CEO demanding that Dennis be re-hired.

My bigger problem, however, was that I had no idea how Dennis ran the department. In reviewing his files, I discovered process after process that did not make any sense to me. His loyal and angry staff was certainly of no help. I was sure I would fail because I had no idea how to do things the way Dennis had done them.

My boss must have seen the panic in my eyes because he asked me one very important question: "Do you know how to do the work? Not necessarily the way Dennis did it, but the actual work itself?" Yes, as a matter of fact, I did. I was well-trained and had the experience to do the work. Whether or not I did the work the same way Dennis did became irrelevant, when I realized that I did not have to fill his shoes. My job was to do the work while wearing my own shoes. Once I realized that, much of my fear was gone.

Lesson Learned: Be yourself! Trying to be someone or something that you are not takes an enormous amount of energy and is rarely a long-term successful strategy. When you take on a new task or a new job at work, don't feel the need to do things like they were done before. Take the opportunity to evaluate processes and procedures and draw upon your own strengths to get the job done right.

MISTAKE #3 – NOT TRUSTING MY INSTINCT

Women are very intuitive, but we often lack the confidence to trust our own intuition. I learned the hard way that you should not ignore your gut feelings.

Case in point: Our company was growing rapidly and we were excited about hiring several new people. Within my own department, we were looking to hire a director who would take over a large part of my responsibility so I could move on to "bigger and better" things.

The new director's ability to lead a team effectively and independently would have a significant impact on my success, so I knew how important this hiring decision was going to be.

Two senior managers whom I highly respected recommended that I interview Maria for the job. They had worked with Maria at a previous company and they believed she would be an excellent candidate.

Typically, I hire people based on instinct and my gut told me that Maria was not the right person for the job. There was nothing lacking in her credentials or her experience, but we just did not click. My colleagues felt strongly that Maria was the right person for the job, and I got caught up in their enthusiasm.

Hiring Maria was not a disaster from day one. It took a few months before the people reporting to her began to complain. I told them to be patient and I worked more closely with Maria to no avail.

Maria never embraced the role in the way that I wanted, expected, or needed her to. Her inability to take ownership of the work meant that I was constantly being pulled back into my old job and not able to focus on my new one. I had failed myself, Maria, and our company by making a bad hiring decision. The only right thing to do now was to correct my mistake.

I met with the senior managers who had recommended her and I shared with them my frustration. They were reluctant for me to remove Maria from her position because they had so strongly endorsed her. However, they respected my judgment.

There was an impressive new rising star who reported to Maria and my intuition told me that she was the right person to take on Maria's job. One of the senior managers agreed to offer Maria a position within his department, but in the end, she elected to leave our organization entirely. The rising star, Rosie, turned out to be one of my top performers, thereby reaffirming my faith in my intuition.

Lesson Learned: Many women have strong intuition that they dismiss when making business decisions. They think that a woman's intuition is not as legitimate as more traditional fact-based methods of decision making.

If you have a history of making good decisions based on your intuition, then by all means, use it. Gut instinct is a very powerful tool, and it would be to our advantage to gain greater comfort in relying on it.

MISTAKE #4 – LETTING MY EGO GET IN MY WAY

High achieving professional women are typically self-confident and driven. We also tend to be competitive, which generally serves us well in working with men in the business world. However, it does have its disadvantages.

When taken to an extreme, intense competition can prevent people from exercising sound judgment. It can drive people to focus on winning at all costs. It can create a situation where the competition becomes extremely personal and egos are on the line. When this happens, the situation moves away from being healthy spirited competition and starts to look more like personal revenge. That's exactly what happened when Reid joined my department.

Case in point: Reid had worked for our company for many years before being assigned to my department. He was a mid-level professional who was not in a management position. He was seen as a superstar in the eyes of one very important client, but that alone seemed insufficient to explain the unusual clout that Reid had within the company.

If there was an exception to any rule, it was Reid. He demanded special privileges and he got them. His power was totally inconsistent with his position on the organizational chart and I never knew why. His power appeared undeserving and unearned.

Unfortunately for me, a company re-organization landed Reid, a handful of his colleagues, and his boss directly into my department. Almost immediately, Reid's actions indicated that he had no intention of changing anything about the way he did his work. If his methods were inconsistent with our department's procedures, then he would simply ignore our procedures.

I was initially stunned by Reid's arrogance and insubordination. I had never and would never be so blatantly disrespectful to someone above me on the organizational chart. Yet, it was clear that Reid was completely comfortable with his behavior which led me to believe that he knew he was exempt from any consequences.

It did not take long for other people in my department to begin to question Reid's special privileges. Why was he permitted to work almost exclusively on only one program when they were required to work on multiple programs? Why was he given flexibility in his work schedule when they were not? Why was he permitted to so blatantly disregard policies and procedures when they had to comply with them?

I could not answer their questions because I did not know the answers myself. I felt as if Reid's special privileges were undermining my ability to be a fair, credible, and effective leader. I turned to Human Resources for help. I solicited their support in establishing my authority over Reid, but they did not provide it. They told me that for all intents and purposes, Reid was untouchable as an employee. They allowed him to hold some unexplainable power over the company and he knew it.

As time went on, things got worse. I felt as if Reid was gloating in his ability to disregard my directives, and he appeared to relish the chance to publicly wield his power over me. As my professional ego took a beating, my competitive nature went into overdrive. I crossed the line from engaging in friendly competition to seeking personal revenge.

I became fixated on wanting to prove my authority over Reid. As a result, I wasted almost a year of intense energy, emotion, and aggravation trying to establish my authority over Reid (which I never did).

In hindsight, I realized that I made a costly mistake in allowing my ego to draw me into a power struggle with a person who had the complete support and backing of upper management. It was a no-win situation from the very beginning, and I should have been wise enough to see that.

Lessons Learned: There will always be people in your organization who receive special privileges for no apparent reason. They are told "yes'" when all other employees are told "no."

If you are anything like me, these people will infuriate you. Their privileges will gnaw at your sense of equity and fairness and you will want to make things right. You can't. You can't bring logic to an illogical situation.

Things will never be fair or equitable at the office; just as they will never be fair or equitable in life. There will always be people who get paid more than their co-workers, produce fewer results than their co-workers, and yield undeserving power and influence over their more deserving co-workers.

For your own sanity, you need to try to accept these things as they are, not as you want them to be. Easy to say, I know, but these strategies might help.

- **Face your emotions head on.** Admit how you feel. Write a letter venting all your irritation and pretend that you are able to send it to the upper managers who support the Reid in your life. Don't hold back. Add to the letter as often as you want to (but never save a copy of it at the office).

- **Distract yourself.** Call a friend who makes you laugh. Talk to her about topics you enjoy. Laughter and distraction are great ways to deflate your irritation.

- **Exercise.** Enjoy the positive impact of those endorphins.

- **Re-claim control over your own emotions.** You may not be able to control the situation at work, but you can control your reaction to the situation. Decide that the Reid in your life has enough undeserved power already and don't let him drain your positive energy.

- **Reward yourself for positive behavior.** When you are able to walk away from a difficult situation with Reid without letting it get the best of you, reward yourself. Make it a big reward or something as small as your favorite candy bar from the company vending machine.

- **Take control of the timing of your interactions.** In other words, don't meet first thing in the morning with someone like Reid when you know it will get your day off to a bad start. Don't feel the need to open an e-mail from him as soon as it arrives in your inbox. Take control of the timing of your interactions and make sure you're in the proper frame of mind before you decide to deal with him.

TO SUMMARIZE

Mistakes are unavoidable. They happen to the best of us. The good news is that smart women rarely make the same mistake twice.

I presented four of my biggest mistakes in this chapter with the hopes of helping you avoid them altogether. I chose these four because they are common mistakes that you are likely to face in your own career.

No one looks forward to making a mistake, but very few mistakes are ever serious enough to derail an otherwise successful career.

Each mistake you make will present you with anopportunity to reflect, then to learn, and finally, to grow if you let it. I am confident that you can find the valuable lessons to be learned from most of your own mistakes, just as I've been able to do for most of mine.

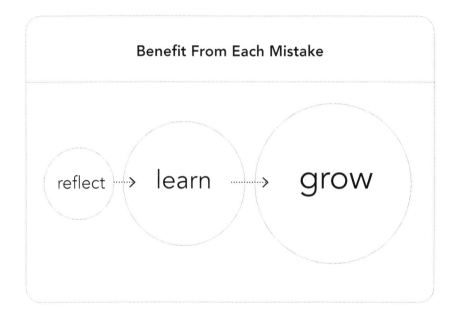

Benefit From Each Mistake

reflect ┄┄> learn ┄┄┄> grow

chapter

15

Managing Your Mommy Guilt

I don't presume to know the details of your life as a working mom, but I do believe I know your major themes:

- Never enough time at work.

- Never enough time at home.

- Never enough time to take care of yourself.

- Multi-tasking just to keep your head above water.

I know first-hand what it's like to juggle a million balls at once – knowing that eventually a few of them are going to fall – hoping that it's not the really important ones that do. I know what it's like to feel like you're never the perfect mother or the perfect employee. I know what it's like to wish that you could, just once, give something your undivided attention.

The truth is that as long as there are working moms there will be mommy guilt. There is comfort in the camaraderie. Expecting to avoid the guilt is almost impossible, but learning how to manage it is within your control.

MY LIFE AS A MOM

By way of introduction, let me tell you a little bit about the two people who call me "mom." My daughter Kate is ten years old. My son Andrew is five. She is smart; he is funny. She is calm; he is not. They are very different in many ways, but they do share one important thing in common. They have never known anything other than life with a working mom.

Like many professional women, I postponed having my first child until my mid-30s. I wanted time to get my career started. Ironically, I received my first major promotion into management just a month before going on maternity leave.

I was almost certain that I planned to return to work after a 12-week maternity leave (the amount of time permitted by law by the Family Medical Leave Act better known as FMLA). In all fairness, a woman may not know for sure what she'll do until after the baby is born. I was as sure as I could be that I planned to return to work full-time.

Kate was born on a cold winter morning. By the next afternoon, I was on the phone from my hospital room checking in with the office. This confirmed what I suspected all along—I planned to be a working mom (who was perhaps a bit work-obsessed).

THE WORST-MOTHER-OF-THE-YEAR COMPETITION

Have you ever had one of those days when you feel like you're the worst mother of the year? A better question might be: how recently have you had one of those days? Not that I mean to turn this into a competition, but I'll put my "worst mother" stories up against yours any day.

- Have you ever missed your child's first birthday because you accepted a last-minute dinner invitation from your boss who just happened to be in from out of town? I have.

- Have you ever left your sick 3-year-old child alone in your company's boardroom all day with a backpack full of snacks and a pile of DVDs? I have.

My list of world's worst mother stories goes on and on, but I picked these examples because they highlight two universal truths about working moms.

TRUTH #1

We have guilt. We probably always will.

When things are running smoothly, we deal with the guilt pretty well, but when there's a crack in the plan, our guilt surfaces. Our most guilt-ridden moments happen when we feel forced to choose between being a good employee and a good mom. These two things should not be mutually exclusive.

When they are, as was the case in the story about my own kids, our guilt escalates. The reality is that working moms don't have a lot of wiggle room in our schedules. Our days are highly structured, which helps us maintain our sanity. Unplanned changes to the schedule can send us into a spiral. Whether it's a last minute business dinner or a sick child, unexpected/unanticipated changes put us in scramble mode. So what do you do when you're in scramble mode? You resort to Truth #2.

TRUTH #2

We need a safety net; a large, well-devised safety net.

We all need a list of people we can count on to help out when things don't go as planned – because you know there will be times when things won't go as planned. You need to decide who the people are who can be there to help you out in a jam. For some that might be family, close friends, co-workers, the emergency nanny hotline, or a variety of other creative resources.

My advice to you is to try to find a safety net that is as guilt-free as possible. If asking your parents or your in-laws for help in a pinch makes you feel guilty, then look for a different safety net. Since I unfortunately live out of state from my parents and in-laws, they are not a realistic last-minute safety net for me. Thankfully, I am extremely fortune to have my friend Ellen and my cousin Carole (both stay-at-home moms) as my local guilt-free safety nets. They respond to my half-crazed last-minute requests for help with complete guilt-free grace. I owe much of my sanity to them. I hope you are fortunate enough to have an Ellen or a Carole in your life. If you're not, look for more formalized safety-nets that can help you maintain your sanity and ease your mommy guilt. Sometimes the best way to create a guilt-free safety net is to make it a business transaction and to keep it separate from your friends and family network.

DEFINING GUILT

Guilt is a powerful emotion that is embedded in societal, cultural, religious, and family norms. Regardless of whether or not guilt has a legitimate source, it is a very real emotion for the people who experience it.

I've identified two different kinds of guilt that I call Type 1 and Type 2 guilt (for lack of more creative names).

Type 1 Guilt: Better known as the "I want to spend more time with my kids" guilt.

This is the guilt I think most people think of when they talk about mommy guilt. Working women with Type 1 guilt feel guilty because they actually *want* to be with their kids more and can't because of the demands of their careers (be those financial or personal).

The bottom line is – if Type 1 moms won the lottery, they'd choose to stop working and be home more with their kids.

Type 2 Guilt: Better known as the "I love my kids, but I don't want to spend more time with them" guilt.

This is the lesser discussed type of guilt for the obvious reason that it makes a person sound like a cold-hearted mother. Women with Type 2 guilt feel guilty because they actually *don't want* to be home more with their kids, but feel like they *should* want to.

The bottom line is – if Type 2 moms won the lottery, they'd feel guilty because they would not want to quit their jobs to be home with their kids full-time. They feel guilty about admitting that they enjoy their careers.

SOURCES OF GUILT

One of the best ways to help manage your guilt is to understand the source of it. By understanding where the guilt comes from, you can take some control over it. For example, you might be more successful in changing your family's perceptions of working moms than you would be in changing society's perceptions of working moms.

Society

Our society sends out very strong messages about what we think moms should be doing and mostly that message says: *Moms should be home raising their children.* Different cultures within our society have their own messages as well, so take into account your own cultural heritage if it contributes to or contradicts the message already being handed to you from our society.

As a social psychologist, I find it really interesting that society has a double-standard for working moms. We've all seen news stories about the working mom who worked three jobs to put food on the table for her kids. We applaud these women who HAVE to work to support their families.

On the flip side, society is very judgmental about women who CHOOSE to work. We don't see positive news stories about the corporate executive who leaves her child with a nanny all day while she runs a profitable division at work. Choosing to work implies tremendous selfishness and our society is not supportive of women's selfishness. In our society, if you are in the position where your income is seen as icing on the cake, then we are even more judgmental about your status as a working mom.

Recently, a working mom I was coaching confessed to me that she finally figured out that she does not work just for the money. She said that she used to rationalize her mommy guilt by saying that she had to work. While her family does need her income in order to maintain the lifestyle they have chosen, she said she finally is able to admit that she gets much more out of work than just the money.

Our society is not entirely comfortable with women who admit they ENJOY working. We can rationalize and support the women who have to work to support their families and who would gladly quit in a minute if they had the choice. But, we don't rally around the women who choose to work because they enjoy it.

Religion

Religion can also play a part in how guilty we feel about being a working mom. Some religions are more guilt-based than others. Think about what impact, if any, your religion has on your mommy guilt.

Family

Family has a very strong impact on the way you feel about being a working mom. How do the people in your family feel about you being a working mom? Are they generally supportive or disapproving? What were your own childhood experiences? Did your mother work outside the home when you were growing up? Did you perceive her career as a positive or negative aspect of your childhood?

Guilt as Disappointing Others

By its very nature, guilt implies a discrepancy between who we think we *should be* and who we actually are - the greater the discrepancy, the greater the guilt. Most of us would probably find self-imposed mommy guilt, even if we lived with our kids alone on a deserted island. But our interaction with others certainly helps to alleviate or exacerbate our mommy guilt. When we feel that we are disappointing others, it adds to our guilt.

EXERCISE

Make a list of the important people in your life. Your list should include people in both your personal and professional life. Below is a suggested list, but feel free to create your own.

1. Yourself
2. Your kids
3. Your spouse/significant other
4. Your parents
5. Your in-laws
6. Your siblings
7. Your friends
8. Your co-workers
9. Your clients
10. Your boss

Next to each name on your list:

- Mark a "D" if you feel like you are **disappointing** this person by being a working mom

- Mark an "S" if this person is generally **supportive** of you as a working mom.

- Mark an "N" if this person is generally **neutral** about you being a working mom.

QUESTIONS

a.   Who are the people most supportive of your role as a working mom?

b.   Who are the people least supportive to you as a working mom?

c.   How do you know you are disappointing the people that you feel you are disappointing? Have they told you directly or do you infer it? Similarly, how do you know you are supported by the people you feel support you? Have they told you or do you infer it?

CHOOSING A SUPPORTIVE NETWORK

I realize I'm stating the obvious, but you should try to surround yourself with people who support you as a working mom. Spend as much time as you can with the supportive people. Supportive people energize you and re-affirm your decisions. Disappointed people drain your energy and undermine your confidence.

At the most successful and sane point in my corporate career, I was fortunate to have six direct reports who formed a very supportive network. Four of them were working moms with young children, one was a working mom with a college-aged child, and one was a working dad with young children.

Most people don't get to choose the people they work with, but take control of your choices as much as you can by spending time with people in your organization who support you as a working mom. Consider organizing an informal network of working moms at your office if one does not already exist.

THE LIFE CYCLE OF GUILT

Guilt generally ebbs and flows. Sometimes it changes by the day, sometimes by the week, month, or year. Understanding the patterns of your guilt, and what triggers your guilt, can help you to manage it more effectively.

EXERCISE

1. Which number on the continuum below best represents your CURRENT mommy guilt?

0 . . . 1 . . . 2 . . . 3 . . . 4 . . . 5 . . . 6 . . . 7 . . . 8 . . . 9 . . . 10

Use the following guilt guide:

1 = "Guilt, what guilt?"

5 = "Yes, I have guilt, but I can deal with it most of the
time."

10 = "The guilt is unbearable."

2. Which number on the continuum below best represents
the LEAST guilt you remember feeling?

0 . . . 1 . . . 2 . . . 3 . . . 4 . . . 5 . . . 6 . . . 7 . . . 8 . . . 9 . . . 10

Use the following guilt guide:

1 = "Guilt, what guilt?"

5 = "Yes, I have guilt, but I can deal with it most of the
time."

10 = "The guilt is unbearable."

3. Which number on the continuum below best represents
the MOST guilt you remember feeling?

0 . . . 1 . . . 2 . . . 3 . . . 4 . . . 5 . . . 6 . . . 7 . . . 8 . . . 9 . . . 10

Use the following guilt guide:

1 = "Guilt, what guilt?"

5 = "Yes, I have guilt, but I can deal with itmost of the time."

10 = "The guilt is unbearable."

SCORING AND REFLECTION

There is no specific scoring for this exercise. Whatever numbers you selected undoubtedly puts you in good company with many other working moms. The purpose of this exercise is to highlight the range of your guilt and to remind you that mommy guilt often fluctuates over time.

- How does your current level of mommy guilt numerically compare to the most mommy guilt you've ever experienced? To the least mommy guilt you've ever experienced?

- Is there a significant difference in your scores between your most and least guilt, or is your level of mommy guilt fairly consistent over time?

- What specific factors trigger mommy guilt for you?

- What successful strategies have you used in the past that can help minimize or reduce any mommy guilt you may be currently experiencing?

A LESS GUILTY MOM IS A MORE SANE MOM

Learning to minimize your mommy guilt is an important part in maintaining your overall sanity. Take time to engage in the activities you listed to replenish your own sanity.

Call it stereotypically female if you want to, but shopping has always been one of my favorite ways to salvage a little sanity. A stolen afternoon away from the office shopping with a female colleague is often more therapeutic than all the traditional corporate team building exercises combined.

For years, men have been playing golf as their way of regaining some sanity on company time and expense. As a society, we've accepted the ritual as a normal and healthy part of the business culture. With more women in positions of power, I am hopeful that the corporate-sponsored shopping spree can't be far off.

THE ALLURE OF PART-TIME WORK

In the workshops I conduct, women overwhelmingly tell me that they crave greater flexibility in their lives. They believe part-time work is their golden ticket to greater sanity.

This, like many other myths, has its downside. How many of you have known of the part-time employee who gets paid part-time to do full-time work? How many women have negotiated part-time work or flexible work arrangements only to have those arrangements never come to fruition? How many moms with Fridays off are in the office on Fridays?

Sue, one of my direct reports negotiated (as part of her acceptance of our job offer) the opportunity to work from home once a week because of her long commute to our office. There was nothing, in theory, that should have prevented Sue from being able to successfully work from home one day a week. In reality, she worked from home less than a dozen times in her seven years with our organization. The reality of the job did not unfold in a way that enabled her to work from home once a week. Her arrangement, like many other part-time or flex-time arrangements that I know of, are better in theory than in reality.

Yet, the part-time job still remains the ideal for many working women. What is keeping us from setting up part-time careers that work for women and employers? The answer to this eludes me, but I suspect it has to do with the male-dominated work culture where we value face-time as much as performance, where hours at the office are worn like a badge of honor, and where we assume our clients expect our constant availability.

I conducted a brief survey with a small sample of working women at various companies in Minneapolis and St. Paul. The women had children ranging in age from newborns to teenagers. I asked them which of the following statements best described their ideal working situation:

a) Not working for pay.

- Chosen by 5% of the women in the survey.

b) Working part-time.

- Chosen by 90% of the women in the survey.

c) Working full-time (approximately 40 hours per week)

- Chosen by 0% of the women in the survey.

d) Working full-time (however many hours it takes to get the job done).

- Chosen by 5% of the women in the survey.

The majority of the women (90%) wanted to work part-time. When I asked them to describe what the ideal part-time situation would look like to them, their answers were as individual as the women themselves. The most creative answer was a year-round cycle of full-time work for three months followed by one month off.

When I asked women why they were not working part-time, they said:

- Full-time work is the nature of the business.

- The company requires it.

- It's hard to find good part-time opportunities.

- I am the primary bread-winner in our family.

- Unplanned emergencies at work always come up and you have to be there for them.

- I'm worried about how I would be treated and respected by my co-workers, if I worked part-time.

- Golden hand-cuffs (salary) keep me working full-time.

- Loss of career track if I don't work full-time.

- Women are marginalized when they work part-time.

- I don't want to work part-time and have my peers become my boss.

- I want the success, the recognition, the money.

Would the business community crumble if more women worked part-time? I don't know the answer to that, but I can tell you that most women believe that they'd be happier and saner if part-time work was an option for them.

In the end, I am both encouraged and frustrated by the progress that some companies and some women are making in regard to flexible work arrangements. *Working Mother* magazine (March, 2008) profiled some amazing entrepreneurs who found great success in creating their own companies that offer flexibility and sanity to working moms.

These are wonderful examples of how life can be, but the reality for most working moms is that these are only examples in a magazine. They don't represent the reality for the average working mom.

Most women do not work for the cutting-edge companies that "get it." Most women are not entrepreneurs. Most women still work for organizations that offer little to no flexibility in their work schedules. How frustrating!

TEN SMALL CHANGES FOR MANAGING YOUR GUILT

Sometimes the best way to manage your guilt is to start by making a few small changes. The following are ten of my favorite small changes:

1. Talk to your child's teacher at the beginning of the school year. Let her know you need to know about school events well in advance. Tell her that you can rarely attend activities that are announced at the last minute. Go over the list and decide which ones are most important to you and your child. Block that time out immediately on your work schedule and stick to it.

2. Find a daycare that you feel really good about – whether that be family, nanny, daycare, or other arrangements. Make sure you have no doubt that your children are safe and well-taken care of so that you do not have to worry about them while you are at work.

3. Make your place of work fun for your kids. Bring them in on weekends. Show them where the paper clips are kept, where the candy dishes are, the copy machine. Let them push the buttons on the elevator.

4. Try not to use phrases such as "Mommy has to go to work now." Instead say something like, "You are

going to do your work now at school and Mommy is going to do her work now at the office. We will each have fun while we miss each other. At the end of the day, we'll have our special time together."

5. At home, outsource those things that occupy your time and do not bring you enjoyment. Shop for your groceries on-line while you're at work and have them delivered to your house. Hire a cleaning lady so that you can play with your kids on the weekend rather than scrub your kitchen floor.

6. Create special memories for your children. They do not have to be big memories like Disney World. Do small things, like a weekly dinner out, with your child. Kids thrive on routine and they really look forward to something they can count on from you.

7. Set aside weekly catch-up time (See Chapter 3 for details).

8. Stay connected with other working moms. Sometimes, all I need is a few minutes to vent with people who understand my stress. When I spend time with other working moms I feel affirmed and energized.

9. Make staying healthy a priority. Guilt is an emotion, so whatever you can do to keep yourself emotionally happy and healthy is going to have an impact on your mommy guilt. Things like exercise, healthy eating, and sleep are all important factors in your emotional well-being. They are usually the first to be sacrificed

by busy working moms, but they are essential for your sanity. Make them a priority.

10. Include your children in making choices. You can't attend every event in your children's lives, so if your children are old enough, have a discussion with them about which events are most important to them and do everything you can to attend those events.

TAKING AN ACTIVE ROLE MANAGING YOUR SANITY

Feeling guilty is a passive process. In other words, you don't have to do a thing and guilt will find its way into your heart and into your brain. Managing your mommy guilt is a very *active process* that takes effort on your part. By default, over-extended, tired, busy working moms don't have time to spare. Managing your guilt does take some planning. Make a conscious decision to get actively involved in the process.

Guilt is a real part of life for most working moms, but the guilt is generally not overwhelming. I don't want to end this chapter with non-guilty women thinking they are some rare exception. In a recent poll I conducted with working moms, the average level of guilt was a 5 ½ on a 1 to 10 scale (answers ranged from 1 to 9). The average score represented "Guilt that I can deal with most of the time."

What this tells us is that if you're a working mom who feels guilty, you are in the company of bright, high achieving professional women and if you are a working mom who does not feel guilty, you are in the company of bright, high achieving professional women.

EXERCISE

Before you end this chapter, list three specific things you can do this week that will make you feel good about yourself as a mom.

1. I will _____

2. I will _____

3. I will _____

Here are a few terrific ideas you can borrow from your fellow working moms.

I will:

- Make special time for my children each night before they go to bed. Read them a story or give them a backrub with a calming aromatherapy lotion.

- Put a little note in my child's lunch box saying "hi" from me.

- Really focus on my child when we're both at home. Put away my Blackberry until after she's gone to bed.

- Let my child sleep-in rather than wake her up early for breakfast. Pack a nutritious breakfast that she can eat in the car on the way to school.

- Occasionally bring my kids to work with me on the weekend.

- Think of things I can outsource so that I can spend more time with my kids.

- Learn to say no to unreasonable work requests (like working over long holiday weekends).

- Talk to other working moms for support.

- Exercise.

- Stay calm. Yell less.

- Make sure the last words my children hear every night is "I love you" even if it means saying it over the phone when I'm not at home.

A BRIEF WORD ABOUT PREGNANCY, ADOPTION, AND MATERNITY LEAVE

Mommy guilt often begins long before your baby is born. Anticipating the day when you will leave your child with a caregiver and return to work can be a source of great guilt for some pregnant working women.

Another source of guilt for many high-achieving working women comes from the realization that motherhood may be perceived by some as a career limiting move. You may no longer be seen as the same high-achieving employee after you become a mother.

A big part of how you feel as a working mom is determined by your relationship with your employer during your pregnancy and during your maternity leave.

In order to make the experience as positive as possible, follow these general guidelines:

- Tell your boss you are pregnant or in the process of adopting. It does not have to be right away, but you don't want her hearing the news through the grapevine.

- Be clear about your expectations regarding your maternity leave and your return to work. If you are uncertain about your intentions to return to work, be honest about that as well.

- Become familiar with your organization's maternity leave policies. How do the policies differ from the realities? In other words, what have other women in your position done with regard to maternity leave? Have they taken 12 weeks leave (as permitted by the Family Medical Leave Act), shorter, or longer time off?

- Build alliances with your co-workers who will cover your work while you're on leave. What can you do to help them now so that you've developed the goodwill for them to help you later on?

- Don't act as if you're the first pregnant woman on the planet. People don't want to hear from you every time the baby kicks or you attend a doctor's appointment.

- Don't share intimate details about the baby's conception, birth, or nursing practices. If you think people want to know, I can promise you – they do not!

- Graciously accept a baby shower if one if offered to you, but don't drop hints for one.

- Try to work as long as possible until your delivery, if your health allows. It's not uncommon for women to work up until the day before the baby is born.

  Some women say that keeping active makes the delivery and recovery process easier.

- Be sensitive to fertility issues among your co-workers. You may never know why some women at work do not have children – whether it's by their choice or not.

- Don't take advantage of your pregnancy. Ask for special accommodations only if you need them to maintain a healthy pregnancy.

- Do bring the baby to the office to meet your co-workers if you can. Being a mother is not something you need to hide. Be proud of your role as a mother and a working woman.

chapter

16

What's Being Female Got to Do With It?

When you picked up this book you probably had many questions in your mind about achieving your professional goals, reaching your leadership potential, managing your busy life, and creating sanity - all at the same time. I hope this book has guided you toward meaningful answers to those questions.

However, one important question still remains: *What's being female got to do with it?*

You don't need a lot of statistical data or a myriad of testimonials to confirm for you what you already know. Being female makes you different from your male colleagues. Sometimes you're better, sometimes you're worse, sometimes you're equal, but you're always different.

At first glance, the differences between working men and women encompass everything from our pay, to our power, to the way our voices are heard, to the way we feel about our safety when we travel alone on a business trip.

At a deeper level, the most significant difference between working men and women is our strong desire to make personal connections with the people with whom we work. We value a collaborative work environment, as much as we value our pay checks. We are more interested in building a team than building an empire.

We are looking for organizations that recognize and respect the complexity of our busy lives. To quote a busy working woman herself, "If you want something done, ask a busy person to do it." (Lucille Ball) There are no busier people on this planet than working women. That's why we get asked to do so many things. Thankfully, we are the masters of multi-tasking which helps us to get them done.

When an organization demonstrates that they value the diversity that women bring to the table, we repay them with steadfast loyalty and unparalleled performance. Diversity means more than having token women who look and act like men in positions of power. Real gender diversity happens when organizations encourage and reward the female perspective at all levels in their organization.

Real gender diversity is no longer just a nod to the woman's movement. It's a smart strategic business decision for many companies. According to a *Catalyst* report released October,

2007, Fortune 500 companies with the highest representation of women board members attained significantly higher financial performance on average, then those with the least representation of women board members.

This report points to a very strong correlation between corporate financial performance and gender diversity. Many companies are competing aggressively to hire the top female talent. They are implementing various gender-specific programs aimed at the advancement and retention of working women.

High-potential, high-performing women are in demand. They have more options than ever before. Companies are looking to gain an endorsement as a preferred place for women to work (See list of "Best Companies for Women to Work For" published by *Forbes* and *Working Mother* magazines).

There is no doubt that women have made significant progress in the business world, but there's still a lot of progress to be made. Women comprise 50% of management, professional and related occupations, but only 2.4% of Fortune 500 CEOs are female. (The *Catalyst:* Pyramid of U.S. Women in Business, April 2008)

The population of female mentors ready to guide and inspire the next generation of female leaders is still less than the demand. My purpose in writing this book is to help meet that demand – to share with women the important lessons I've learned throughout my career.

My intent has never been to teach women how to become men, but rather to guide women toward their own greatness. I hope I have done that for you.

FINAL THOUGHTS

I told you at the beginning of this book that the life you imagine for yourself is possible. I believe strongly in the limitless capabilities of working women. I think there is nothing we can not do if we put our minds to it.

I encourage you to start becoming today the person that you wish to be tomorrow.

- Commit to being a professional woman who stays true to her core values.

- Commit to discovering your own greatness.

- Commit to making a difference in the lives of the next generation of female leaders.

- Commit to becoming successful without becoming a man.

Best of luck! If you have time, please share your success and sanity stories with me at www.leadhership1.com.

Appendix A
CHAPTER REVIEWS

Take-Away Messages

CHAPTER 1

- "Having it all" is not about reaching for someone else's ideal. It's not aboutliving up to someone else's expectations. It's about integrating who you are as a person and who you are as a professional into one successful and sane life.

CHAPTER 2

- Success = Your ability to achieve your career goals

- Sanity = Your ability to truly enjoy your life!

- Only you can decide what's important to you. Your success and sanity are largely dependent upon how closely your goals match up with your current reality.

CHAPTER 3

- Set limits on your time: Don't let a project dictate how much time you spend on it.

- Carve out catch-up time: Both you work and your personal life need it.

- Reassess your expectations: You can't be all things to all people all the time.

CHAPTER 4

- Integrity is everything.

- Confidentiality is key.

- Your positive attributes need to outweigh your negative ones.

- Never let your boss be blindsided.

- Companies have financial responsibilities.

CHAPTER 5

- It's never too early or too late to make smart career choices. Part of making smart choices involves a reality-check, an honest evaluation of your skills and abilities compared to the qualities companies value most.

CHAPTER 6

- We can make choices about the size of the pond that we choose to swim in and the size of the fish that we want to be.

- Every woman has power and influence over her own life even if she lacks power and influence over the company in which she works.

- Women are inherently loyal, and we can get trapped by our own loyalty.

CHAPTER 7

- Anyone who tells you that your position on the organizational chart does not matter is undoubtedly a few degrees higher on the chart than you are. It's always the people at the top telling everyone else that they should not worry about their position.

CHAPTER 8

- Corporate culture is the one variable you can't control that has more influence on your success, sanity and overall day-to-day satisfaction at work than any other variable you will encounter.

- If an organization's culture is a good fit for you your talents will shine. If it's not a good fit, your talents (as brilliant as they might be) will be overlooked and undervalued.

CHAPTER 9

- A substantial number of highly qualified women voluntarily leave their careers for a period of time (37%).

- With that said, declining increased responsibility or turning down a promotional opportunity is considered a career ending move in most organizations.

- Corporate America is not ready for high achieving leaders who choose sanity over success.

- Look for precedents set by other women in your organization if there comes a time when you want, or need, a break from the linear career path. Be realistic in your expectations of how your organization might respond to your request.

CHAPTER 10

- A good job in a bad company inevitably turns into a bad job in a bad company.

- Most high achieving women do not stay for very long in a company that they dislike, no matter how much they like their actual job.

CHAPTER 11

- There is strength in discovering and re-discovering your interests throughout your life. What seemed like the perfect career choice at one point, may not feel right today. It's hard to enjoy your success if you feel trapped in an inauthentic career.

CHAPTER 12

- Change is the name of the game. Whether it's you changing jobs or your company making changes, your ability to be successful in times of change comes down to one important factor – your attitude.

CHAPTER 13

- More than any other single attribute, working women are looking for leaders who inspire them. They want a leader who will help them stretch, grow and achieve beyond what they imagined for themselves.

- Second on their list is integrity. They want leaders they can trust, respect and admire.

CHAPTER 14

- Leadership is not a popularity contest.

- Be yourself!

- Women have strong intuition that they dismiss in making business decisions.

- Don't let people who irritate you sap your energy.

CHAPTER 15

- Guilt is not overwhelming for most moms.

- Working moms need a well-devised safety net in place.

- Some mothers feel guilty because they are not home with their children as much as they'd like to be.

- Other mothers feel guilty because they don't want to be home more with their children.

CHAPTER 16

- The most significant difference between working men and women is our strong desire to make personal connections with the people with whom we work.

- Women would rather build a team than an empire.

- Research suggests a correlation between strong corporate financial performance and greater gender diversity.

- Challenge yourself to become the person you imagine you can be.

Appendix B
RECOMMENDED READING LIST

Thank goodness for on-line book stores. They allow me to actually buy a book *about work* while I am still sitting *at work* (now that's the epitome of multi-tasking.)

Of course, buying a book and reading a book are two different things. As a busy working woman, I tend to be better at the former than the latter. But, I have read my fair share of business books. I'd much rather curl up with the hottest new business book than the latest and greatest work of fiction.

The list of best-selling business books is never ending. The list of best- selling business books written specifically *for* women is much shorter. As a professional woman, I appreciate the opportunity to read books that reflect a female perspective. I feel a unique connection with books that are written *for* women in business *by* women in business. These books offer a point of view that is not well represented in the mainstream business literature today.

My current favorite business books are listed below in alphabetical order by title.

The downside to providing a recommended reading list is that I have not read every outstanding book that should legitimately be on my list. In addition, new books will come out that I want to add long before this book is even published.

With those limitations in mind, I recommend my favorite "books of the moment" here with the intention of keeping the list updated at **www.leadhership1.com.**

BOOKS

Basic Black: The Essential Guide for Getting Ahead at Work and in Life By Cathie Black (2007)

- Don't assume that this book should only be read by women seeking the corner office, just because Ms. Black is an accomplished corporate President herself. Her advice is down to earth and applicable for professional women at every level in an organization. I found myself wanting to apply for a job at Hearst Magazines just to work with Cathie Black. She's the smart, insightful, and funny mentor that we all wish we had.

Harvard Business Review on Women in Business – from the HBR Paperback series (2005).

- This book is a compilation of eight articles originally published in Harvard Business Review (HBR). I have not seen a more recent release of this book, but I continue to find articles relevant to women's issues periodically in HBR.

- For additional articles visit **www.hbr.com.** and search for author Sylvia Ann Hewlett. Dr. Hewlett, the founding president for the Center for Work-Life Policy, has written several outstanding articles on issues facing working women. Most notably, Dr. Hewlett co-authored a HBR Research Report titled "The Hidden Brain Drain" which explores the disturbing trend of large numbers of qualified women dropping out of mainstream careers.

*How She Does It: How Women Entrepreneurs
Are Changing the Rules of Business Success*
By Margaret Heffernan (2007).

- This book is at the very top of my "try to
find-time to read this" list. Heffernan, a
five time CEO herself, articulates what it
means to lead from a female perspective
better than any other book I've ever read.
She interviewed hundreds of women
entrepreneurs and she shares her
observations of them in this brilliantly
written book. You will be inspired and
proud to be the best female leader you can
be after reading her book.

Leadership – inspire, liberate, achieve By Tom Peters (2005)

- Thank you, Tom Peters! A business woman
could never be as brazenly pro-female
as Mr. Peters is, without facing enormous
criticism. It's worth picking up this book
for Chapter 3 alone. Where else can you
read one of the top management gurus of
our time make statements like "As leaders,
women rule," "Fire all male salespeople,"
and 'Tomorrow belongs to women."

Play Like A Man Win Like A Woman By Gail Evans (2000).

- For a long time I avoided this book simply because the title seemed to contradict my own philosophy about working women. When I finally read it, I felt an immediate connection with Gail Evans. Her enthusiasm and knowledge of the issues facing working women comes across loud and clear. Evans does an excellent job of explaining how and why men behave the way they do in business. This kind of insight and understanding into the male psyche is very helpful to working women.

Why Women Should Rule the World By Dee Dee Myers (2008).

- The title of this book alone should be enough to make you want to buy it. While the content is definitely heavy on political references, Myers delivers her message in a refreshingly humble and humorous way. Her story of life as President Bill Clinton's Press Secretary is a perfect example of how bright and outwardly successful women still struggle behind the scenes to gain the respect and acceptance they deserve in a male-dominated work environment.

Why Work Sucks and How To Fix It By Cali Ressler and Jody Thomspon (2008)

- This book tells the story of the Results-Only-Work-Environment (ROWE) established by the authors at Best Buy. It is a persuasive account of what can happen when a corporate culture shifts to caring more about results than time spent at the office. ROWE is a dream-come-true for high achieving working women who can out perform their colleagues, but can't compete with them on office "face time." The authors do a great job of demonstrating how an organization that has the right cultural fit for you can have enormous impact on both your success and your sanity.

A WORD ABOUT BOOKS TARGETING WORKING MOMS

There are a number of books written specifically for working moms. They have very catchy titles and colorful covers. I own quite a few of them. The problem I have with most of them is that the tone of the book is either too light-hearted (as in witty with no substance), too touchy-feely (as in therapy with a group hug) or too heavy-hearted (as in emotional anguish for the working women who longs to be home with their children).

While these scenarios may accurately depict the experience of some working moms, it does not reflect my own. For that reason, I do not have many books to recommend in this category, but I've listed one, and I continue to look for others.

How She Really Does It: Secrets of Successful Stay-At-Work Moms By Wendy Sachs. 2005.

Sachs, a highly accomplished writer, successful freelance television producer, and working mom delivers an important message in this book: Work is good for women, from our heads to our souls! She combines relevant statistics, references from the literature and her own personal experience into one humorous and poignant book that I think all working moms would enjoy.

Be careful not to confuse this book with "How She Does It." Both are on this recommended reading list, but this one is specifically for working moms and the other one is not.

MAGAZINES

Books are fantastic, but it's hard to beat the convenience of a quick, easy-to-read magazine. Who doesn't grab a couple magazines for the airplane when you're headed out on a business trip?

I'll never forget the time I was seated next to a burly top male executive in our company on a flight home from our corporate headquarters in Baltimore. When the plane took off, he reached into his briefcase and pulled out the customary stack of reading materials.

Much to my surprise his stack consisted of *People, Star* and *In Touch* magazines. He did not merely skim these magazines, but read each one cover-to-cover. My opinion of him changed immediately (for the better) and my mental image of him mesmerized by the latest Hollywood gossip still makes me smile.

Realistically, the female executive reading the exact same stack of magazines would be more likely to elicit an eye roll from her male colleagues than a smile. So, if you're looking to protect your professional image with a little bit meatier and more credible reading material, let me suggest the following two magazines:

1. *Pink*

- This magazine is my top pick in magazines devoted to professional women. You might not get that from its name. Pink is the one business magazine that consistently has information that I find interesting and relevant to my life as a working woman. The content is definitely focused on high-achieving professional women. It is not readily available at most local newsstands, but a yearly subscription (12 issues) is available at **www.pinkmagazine.com.**

2. *Working Mother*

- For years I've subscribed to Working Mother magazine and if you're a working mom, I suggest you get a subscription, too. Twelve issue per year are available at **www.workingmother.com.** The content is sometimes less career-focused and more mom-focused than I'd like it to be, but I always feel re-connected to working moms when I'm done reading it.

NATIONAL ORGANIZATIONS

1. Catalyst (www.catalyst.org)

- Founded in 1962, Catalyst is the leading nonprofit membership organization working globally with businesses and the professions to build inclusive workplaces and expand opportunities for women and business. If you are not familiar with their work yet, you'll want to be.

- Membership is at the organizational, not the individual level.

2. NAFE (www.Nafe.com)

- The National Association for Female Executives (NAFE) was founded in 1972. The organization has a rich history of providing education, networking, and public advocacy to empower its members to achieve career success and financial security. Members are female executives, women business owners, and others who are committed to NAFE's mission: the advancement of women in the workplace.

- Individual membership gives you access to a biweekly e-newsletter and other NAFE publications.

Appendix C
ACKNOWLEDGEMENTS

This book would not be a sincere representation of success, sanity, leadership, and life without thanking the special people who make these four components possible for me.

My academic mentors Dr. Mark Chesler and Dr. Richard Nault, and my professional mentors Kevin Brueggeman and John Ficken. Each of you encourage me to be true to who I am, and your wisdom and guidance have been instrumental in shaping my career.

My colleagues on the senior leadership team at Experior Assessments: Mark Caulfield, Jill Collins, Brad Hansen, Karen Kendall, Paul Karpinko, and Dan Luk. Together, we experienced what I believe are the best times that any company has ever offered a group of executives.

My dream team: Nikki Shepherd Eatchel, Deb Ringwelski, Sue Steinkamp, Rosie Tolliver, Rob vonKampen, and Lauren Wood. You guys are amazing! Being your boss was the best job I ever had.

Special thanks to Nikki and Sue who have been with me on my professsional journey for a very long time. To quote a line from my favorite musical *Wicked*, "Whatever way our stories end, I know you have re-written mine by being my friend."

Terri Foley, my editor, who held my feet to the fire to make my publishing deadline, and my book designer Heather Griffin. Thank you both for taking my written word and making it so much better.

Pat O'Brien for being the first to suggest that I write a book, and for knowing that this should be its title the minute the phrase came out of my mouth.

Tony Eatchel, Denise Reflexia, and Mike Steinkamp for their tremendous technical and creative assistance.

Sharon Davis (my sister-in-law) who graciously responded to my requests for help with lightening speed and valuable perspective.

To a very special group of women who are always there for me as cheerleaders, healthclub companions, devil's advocates, and professional colleagues: Kristin Englund,

Paige Haensel, Patricia Jorgenson, Andrea Kao, Ellen Konstan, Margaret Vitullo, Carole Schram, Fran Tashjian, Colleen Wilson, Sara Richey, Donna Sue Sunday, Kay Talwar, and Susan Thornton.

My beautiful and courageous cousin Denise Thornton whose perspective on life and death will forever be an inspiration to our family.

My incredibly supportive in-laws, Dr. M.V. and Elizabeth Ali. Thank you for raising a son who does not expect his wife to cook, clean, or do laundry for him.

My husband and my children who share in the dedication of this book. You are my foundation from which I pursue my professional passions.

My phenomenal parents, DonnaLou and David Davis. You sent me off to Kindergarten with the belief that a woman can become successful without becoming a man. I love you for that, and so much more.

Finally to my brother Donn Davis who personifies personal success. I am grateful for your never-ending encouragement. You are the best big brother that a little sister could hope for.

Appendix D
ABOUT THE AUTHOR

Susan Davis-Ali grew up in Cincinnati, Ohio. She earned a BA from Miami University in Oxford, Ohio in 1986, and a PhD in Social Psychology from the University of Michigan, Ann Arbor in 1992.

Over the next decade, Dr. Davis-Ali was a successful corporate executive in the test publishing industry. She was a respected leader in the field and invited speaker at numerous national conferences.

In 2005, Dr. Davis-Ali left the testing industry to pursue her passion for women's leadership. She founded Leadhership1, Inc., a professional coaching company committed to helping working women achieve success and sanity in their lives. She is currently the President of Leadhership1. Her coaching philosophy reflects her academic background as well as her real life experiences as a corporate executive.

She enjoys her own success and sanity in St. Paul, Minnesota with her husband, their two children, and their dogs. You can contact her at **www.leadhership1.com.**

Made in the USA
Lexington, KY
23 December 2010